100 STRANGEST

UNEXPLAINED

MYSTERIES

MATT LAMY

Capella

Published by Arcturus Publishing Limited

For AG City Books

This edition printed in 2004

Copyright © 2003 Arcturus Publishing Limited
26/27 Bickels Yard, 151–153 Bermondsey Street, London SE1 3HA

British Library Cataloguing-in-Publication Data: a catalogue
record for this book is available from the British Library

ISBN 1-84193-168-3

Typeset by Mike Harrington at MATS

Printed in China

CONTENTS

PUZZLING PEOPLE AND ENIGMATIC ENTITIES 151

SECRET SOCIETIES AND HIDDEN TREASURES 175

MISCELLANEOUS 193

BEASTS & MONSTERS

THE BEAST OF BODMIN

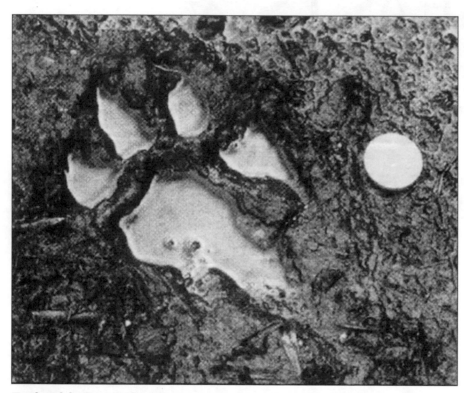

Tracks of the Beast? The ten pence coin shows the scale of this paw-print

THE BEAST OF BODMIN: whether it is a native cat, previously thought extinct, or an escaped exotic pet, the Beast of Bodmin is a creature that refuses to disappear. Indeed, sightings of the panther-like creature continue apace and, unlike other mysterious beasts, modern technology is actually helping to prove its existence. Bodmin Moor is an area of National Park land in Cornwall, southwest England. Since 1983 there have been over sixty sightings of big cats in the area, and some experts suggest there may be a whole breeding population on the moors. In fact, one recent sighting was of a mother cat and her cub together. Despite wide-ranging testimonials from reliable witnesses, a British government report in 1995 concluded that there was no evidence of big cats on the moors.

However, since 1995 some quite startling, tangible evidence has been produced. A 20-second video released in July 1998 clearly shows a large black animal roaming the moor. Experts believe the footage is the best evidence yet to support the idea that big cats are living in the area. Many also suggest the beasts may be a native species of cat which was thought to have become extinct over a hundred years ago. Around the time of the video release, Maurice Jenkins, a quarry weighbridge worker was driving near Exmoor, near Bodmin, when he spotted an odd beast at the side of the road. He trained his car headlights on the creature.

'It was a big black pussycat. His eyes reflected in my headlights and I slowed down so I could get a better look and it sat watching me. It was the size of a collie dog with jet-black head and tail. He leapt away and made off into the fields,'

Jenkins said afterwards.

Real biological evidence has also been found in recent years. A large skull with huge fangs was found near the River Fowley on Bodmin Moor. The bones were sent to mammal specialists at the British Natural History Museum who, when they examined it, realised that the skull did not belong to a creature normally found in the English countryside. Because of the size and position of the teeth, they also deduced that it was the head of a large cat.

In November 1999 a spate of farm animal mutilations on Bodmin Moor caused a high-tech option to be introduced in finding the beast. A calf and two sheep were attacked and ripped apart by some unknown creature, so an infrared video camera, activated by movement, was installed in a secret location on the moor. Similarly, in January 2001, reserve volunteers from a nearby Royal Air Force base used state-of-the-art night-vision military equipment to hunt for the creature. Rather than practise exercises against imaginary foe, RAF commanders thought that it would be more interesting for the troops to look for the fabled Beast of Bodmin.

Certainly, the idea of strange big cats roaming Britain is not totally bizarre. In May 2001, a peculiar, vicious-looking wild animal was found in the garden of a house in Barnet, north London. A huge team of armed police, RSPCA inspectors and vets were needed to capture what turned out to be a lynx. A similar event happened in September 1998 when people living close by, in Potters Bar and South Mimms, were told to stay indoors whilst police looked for a large cat sighted there. Generally, however, such animals pose little threat to the human population.

Farmers in southwest England do not agree that these creatures are so benign, and many sceptics believe the Beast of Bodmin is, if anything, an escaped foreign cat. A number go missing from zoos and wildlife parks each year, and Britain's 1976 Dangerous Wild Animals Act made ownership of exotic big cats illegal. Some people believe that if such a pet were to escape from a private collection, its owner would be hesitant to report it missing. Whatever the truth about its origin, there is growing, indisputable evidence that a large, black, feral cat is stalking the land of Bodmin Moor.

The Beast strikes again; or is it in fact a fox with a rabbit?

BIGFOOT

IN THE WILDS OF NORTH AMERICA a mystical ape-like creature hides in the shadows. Standing over seven feet tall and having an immense, muscled body, it should be hard to stay concealed. Many that see him say he just disappears into the background. Like a man, he walks upright, but the short black hair covering his entire body indicates he is no homo-sapien. No bodies, bones or remains have ever been found despite more than two centuries of searching. The only evidence we have of this mythical beast is its huge tracks. That is why the creature is named 'Bigfoot'.

Like many legendary Native American monsters, Bigfoot is a central part of indigenous traditional tales. They call him 'Sasquatch,' the 'hairy giant of the woods.' But it was his early personal introduction to European settlers that sparked off real interest. In 1811, David Thompson, a white trader, was in the north Rocky Mountains when he spotted a set of massive fourteen by eight-inch footprints. Over many years, the tales of Sasquatch spread and on 4th July 1884, the Daily Colonist newspaper in British Columbia was proud to announce that a train crew had caught a strange beast. In reality, the stocky, black-haired primate that they trapped was probably just a chimpanzee.

The American and Canadian mountains gradually grew awash with stories of Sasquatch appearances; there were even of reports of gangs of strange creatures attacking people in the forests. The Sasquatch phenomenon was never solely focused on the idea of a single creature, and people have always considered there might be a breeding colony. At that time, the mystical beasts were primarily of interest to lumberjacks, miners and those who lived or worked in areas where it had been sighted.

That changed in 1958 when Jerry Crew, a bulldozer operator working in Humboldt County, California, made casts of the bizarre footprints he had found. A local newspaper photographed Crew, and his picture was syndicated across the United States. This sight of a man holding a plaster cast record of the tracks of a mysterious beast started the modern Bigfoot legend. But if Crew's discovery helped to launch the myth, it was an episode nine years later that sealed Bigfoot's place in the American consciousness.

In October 1967, Roger Patterson and Bob Gimlin were riding on horseback through Bluff Creek, north California. They were in the area specifically looking for Bigfoot. Suddenly one appeared in their path, and Patterson was thrown from his horse. Whilst Gimlin kept a rifle trained on the beast, Patterson quickly regained his footing and ran towards the creature, filming all the time with a cine camera they had taken with them. The result is perhaps the most enigmatic evidence yet. The footage shows a large hairy biped slowly strolling into the undergrowth. Experts who have closely studied the film suggest it is a female Bigfoot, as two mammary glands are just discernible on its front.

Although the evidence is startling, many have questioned its authenticity. Some experts believe, if the film is played at a slightly faster speed, it could easily be a human in a costume. However, aspects of the footage are quite amazing. For example, biotechnology scientists have said that for a

A larger-than-life – we hope! – model of Bigfoot on display outside a US museum.

creature like Bigfoot to walk upright it would need an extended heel. The creature on the film has an extended heel.

Experts in the industry initially expected the film merely to be special effects, but they have been unable to find any tell-tale signs that it is a hoax. Similarly, a group of Russian scientists who attempted to determine the correct speed of the film came to the conclusion that the creature really did have a long, lumbering gait. However, Gimlin himself has entertained the possibility that

5

Still taken from Roger Patterson's film of Bigfoot.

he might have been an unwitting participant in a hoax orchestrated by his friend. This we shall never know as Patterson died of cancer in 1972.

More recent sightings of the ape-man have taken on a new and bizarre twist. People have reported seeing UFOs in the regions of Bigfoot appearances. Also, the creatures are now said to have bright red eyes and be carrying glowing orbs. This may seem a strange development, but Sasquatches were always reported as having a quality beyond the physical, and it had always been suggested that when they die, Bigfoot bodies vanish into the ether. This is a shame, because to really accept Bigfoot's presence, the world needs to see some hard, physical evidence.

THE BIG GREY MAN

IN THE SCOTTISH HIGHLANDS lies a mountain where many have felt a dread quite unlike anything else they have ever experienced. As the fogs and mists roll across the cairns, they say there lurks a creature huge and terrifying. They call it 'Am Fear Liath Mor,' or the 'Big Grey Man.' Some see him as an old figure in robes, a giant, or even a devil. The creature does not just threaten with a force of physical power, this beast also exudes an almost suicidal sense of depression and panic in all who come near it.

Ben MacDhui is the second highest mountain in Scotland, standing at over 4,000 feet. It is an imposing sight and a substantial test for experienced climbers. Many of the witnesses who see, or feel the presence of, the Grey Man are serious, hardened mountaineers, not prone to flights of fancy.

The first person to reveal he had met the mountain's strange tenant was Professor Norman Collie. Collie was a respected and well known climber, but when he gave his speech to the Cairngorm Club in 1925, the audience was truly stunned.

Collie explained that he had been coming down from the peak of Ben MacDhui in 1891 when he heard footsteps behind him. At first, shrouded in mist, he rationalised that it must just have been an echo of his own footfalls. But eventually he realised the noises he heard were not corresponding to the movements he was making. It sounded like a giant was following him. He said it was

'as if someone was walking after me, but taking steps three or four times the length of my own.'

Terrified, Collie blindly ran for four or five miles down the mountainside until he could no longer hear the noise. Collie never returned to the mountain, and to his dying day resolutely believed there was, 'something very queer about Ben MacDhui.'

During the Second World War, Peter Densham was a mountain rescue worker, locating and saving pilots who had crashed in the Cairngorms. One day he was at the top of Ben MacDhui when a heavy mist started to fall. He sat and waited for conditions to improve. After a while he began to hear strange crunching noises and suddenly felt a presence close by. He stood up to investigate, but was immediately seized by a feeling of panic. Before he realised what was happening, he was running down the mountain, dangerously close to the sheer cliff edge. He said afterwards 'I tried to stop myself and found this extremely difficult to do. It was as if someone was pushing me. I managed to deflect my course, but with a great deal of difficulty.'

Since then, many people have spotted a strange being, or felt an overpowering sense of impending doom in the area. One of the most recent encounters occurred in the early 1990s. Three men were walking in a forest just outside Aberdeen. One of the party spotted a human-shaped figure running across the track a little way ahead of them. He told his friends, and when they all looked in the same direction they saw a strange, not-quite-human face. A few weeks later, the same group were driving in the area when they realised they were being followed by the same tall, dark being. The creature kept pace, even at speeds of 45 miles an hour, but eventually tired and stopped. Again, these men felt a distinct sense of terror and foreboding.

Monster enthusiasts have plenty of ideas about the beast's origin. Some say he could be an alien, or the ghost of an old Highland race, or even a mystical, wise religious figure. One interesting theory is that atop Ben MacDhui there is a gateway to another dimension, and this creature is the gatekeeper. If this really is his role, then he is doing a good job. After an experience with the Big Grey Man, very few people have dared to venture up Ben MacDhui again.

Tarn in the foothills of the mountain of Ben Macdhui.

The Loch Ness Monster

OF ALL THE MYTHICAL BEASTS in the world, the most famous, most hunted for, and most talked about must be 'Nessie' the Loch Ness Monster. She, for the Scottish monster is always seen as a not-so-wee lassie, is often the first phenomenon thought about when the subject of unexplained mysteries is raised. She is an internationally-known celebrity, who has probably done more for her native tourist industry than any other famous Scot. There have been Nessie documentaries, pro-grammes, films and even cartoons. But although she appears each year to a select few, she has been too shy to debut in a major scientific investigation. So is Nessie really a strange creature, lost in time, and lurking at the bottom of Loch Ness?

Loch Ness is a 24-mile-long freshwater lake found in the Great Glenn, a massive crevice that cuts the Scottish Highlands in two. The loch is up to a thousand feet deep and, at some points, a mile-and-a-half wide. The first tale of a monster living in the water originates in 565AD and features Saint Columba, who rescued a swimmer from the beast's advances. Experts now generally feel that Saint Columba actually encountered a known, normal, marine animal that had ended up outside its natural environment. Although the loch continued to be the focus of strange sightings, it was not until the 20th century that the phenomenon really flourished.

Loch Ness, Scotland. Could this be the home of a plesiosaur?

In 1933 the Loch Ness Lakeshore road was built. This initiated a flood of sightings and created the Nessie legend. In April that year, a local couple spotted an enormous animal rolling and playing in the water. They reported what they had seen to the man in charge of salmon stocks in the loch who then saw the monster himself, describing it as having a six-feet-long neck, a serpentine head and a huge hump. He suggested the creature was a total of 30 feet in length. In the July a family from London were driving along when they almost crashed into a massive dark, long-necked animal that strolled across their path and then disappeared into the water. Similarly, early the next year a young veterinary student was riding his motorcycle along the road when he almost struck a creature. He said what he saw had a large bulky body, with flippers, a long neck and a small head.

Over the years, many people have tried to capture the creature on film. One Nessie witness managed to take a rather inconclusive photograph of something appearing from the water in 1933. In 1934 a London doctor released a most mysterious photograph of the monster to the public. It showed a strange head and neck appearing from the water; 60 years later it was revealed to be a fake. In April 1960 an aeronautical engineer used a 16mm movie camera to film something moving through the loch's waves. Although it has never been established exactly what is captured on the film, experts at the Royal Air Force's photographic department have verified that the footage is not a fake and has not been tampered with. Dinsdale himself devoted the rest of his life to finding Nessie.

Recent years have also provided new sightings. In June 1993, a couple were on the bank of the loch when they saw a huge, strange creature lolling about in the water. They said it must have been about 40-feet-long, with a giraffe-like neck and very light brown flesh. Later that same evening, a father and son were on their way home when they spotted something odd in the water. They later told reporters they saw an animal with a neck like a giraffe swimming swiftly away from the shore. Because of the evidence accrued during these two episodes, bookmakers William Hill slashed the odds of there really being a Loch Ness Monster from 500-1 to 100-1.

Despite over 3,000 similar sightings by private individuals, Nessie has always been coy about exposing herself to dedicated, scientific research teams. The Academy of Applied Science from Boston, Massachusetts operated the first extensive expedition in the early 1970s. Using underwater cameras and

The first photo of the Loch Ness Monster, which sparked the current 'Nessiemania'.

sonar equipment, the project captured images of what looked like an eight-feet-long flipper, an unusual 20-feet-long aquatic body, and even a hazy photo of a creature's face. However, an organised, structured sonar sweep of the loch in 1987, named 'Operation Deepscan,' revealed the earlier portrait picture of Nessie was actually a tree stump. That said, Deepscan did report various, unaccounted-for, large sonar echoes moving about in the extreme depths of the loch.

Although these hunts have proved inconclusive, other recent scientific evidence has been more hopeful. In March 2000, a team of Norwegian scientists, the Global Underwater Search Team, picked up bizarre noises in the loch's water. At one point whatever was making the sound even crashed into the team's underwater microphone. This group had already recorded unusual sounds from another mythically monster-infested lake in Norway. The strange noises found in Loch Ness are described as a cross between a snorting horse and an eating pig, closely matching the experiences in Norway. Not only does this suggest there are unknown creatures in both lakes, but they might actually be related. In recent years, sonar equipment has also discovered huge underwater caverns opening onto the bottom

Monster hunters: the search for Nessie goes on.

of the loch. These structures have been termed 'Nessie's Lair,' and may well be large enough to house and hide a whole family of monsters.

It is agreed that a breeding colony of beasts would be needed to continue its existence, and some witness accounts have reported more than one Nessie appearing on the water's surface. Nessie's actual species is still unknown although experts have suggested it may be a manatee or type of primitive whale. It my also be a large otter, a long-necked seal, a huge eel, or even a giant walrus. However, Nessie seems to bear a much stronger resemblance to a creature now thought to be extinct. This is called the plesiosaur, a marine dinosaur that has not been found on Earth for over 60 million years. It had large flippers, a small head and a large body, and some experts

believe a few of these animals were stranded in the loch after the last Ice Age.

None of these suggestions are completely plausible. Even if the plesiosaur did survive the disaster that wiped out the rest of its fellow prehistoric creatures, it is generally believed to be a cold-blooded animal, and would find the chilly environment of a Scottish lake too cold to survive. If Nessie is really a modern day aquatic mammal like a whale or a seal, then it would constantly have to come to the surface for air, resulting in many more sightings. One cannot help but feel there might actually be something in the murky depths of Loch Ness. With a continued interest that actually grows with each unsuccessful scientific study, this loch remains the home of the world's most mysterious, unexplainable monster.

THE LUSCA & ST AUGUSTA PHENOMENA

'WE KNOW MORE ABOUT the surface of the moon than we do about the bottom of our deepest oceans,' so the old saying goes. It is an adage that, over time, is proving more and more relevant. What creatures actually do lurk at the bottom of the sea? Around the Bahamas and the southeast American coast there are tales of a giant octopus that captures unwary swimmers and small boats. The people of the islands call it the 'Lusca' and believe it lives in deep underwater caves. However, no one has ever seen the creature in it natural environment and lived to tell the tale.

One evening in November 1896 two men were cycling along the coast just outside their hometown of St Augustine, Florida. As they looked over the beach, they noticed a huge carcass. It was 23 feet long, 18 feet wide, four feet high, and it seemed to have multiple legs. The two men decided to tell Dr Dewitt Webb, the founder of the St Augustine Historical Society and Institute of Science, who came to examine the corpse.

Webb photographed the body, noting it was a silvery pink colour, and took samples. Webb recorded that the skin was axe-proof, being three and a half inches thick. He also estimated that the body weighed around six or seven tonnes. It needed four horses and a whole team of people from the local community to drag it the painstaking 40 feet up the beach in order to keep it away from the rolling waves.

Webb was convinced it was not part of a whale, and must have been some kind of unknown giant octopus, so he sent letters describing the carcass to many eminent scientists. One such expert was Professor Verrill at the National Museum (now called

The immense body of an octopus, washed up on the Florida shore. Is this the real Kraken?

the Smithsonian) in Washington DC. Verrill stated that the creature was actually a squid. When Webb sent him more information, he changed his mind and said it was an octopus. Verrill suggested it probably had tentacles around 100 feet long.

Verrill refused to see the dead creature in person, or indeed to provide any funds or resources to help preserve the sea monster.

Even so, the professor decided this new species should be named after himself, calling it 'Octopus Giganteous Verrill.' Finally, he changed his mind again after receiving tissue samples, and said the body was probably just the head of a sperm whale. Webb was disappointed and preserved as many samples of the creature as he could. Eventually the corpse was retaken by the sea.

Over fifty years later, two marine biologists, Dr F.G.Wood and Dr J.F.Gennaro Jr., discovered stories of the St Augustine sea monster in old newspaper clippings. They applied to the Smithsonian and took samples from the original specimens Webb had sent Verrill. Wood had worked in the Bahamas and knew of the famous 'Lusca.' The legend said that it was a giant octopus, with arms seventy-five feet long, that lived in great deep blue holes in the sea floor. By looking at the samples, Wood and Gennaro were able to deduce that the body was indeed that of an enormous octopus. At long last, Webb had been proved right.

In recent years other examples of huge, previously unknown, sea creatures have been discovered. Tales of giant squid have been told through the ages, but it is only in the last century that accurate and scientific details have been truly kept. Even in this day and age, some bizarre stories still have crop up. French fishermen have recently been attacked by one multi-legged sea creature, and marine biologists are constantly finding remains of squid which out-size the previously known largest.

At the moment, the biggest giant squid find happened in April 2003 when a colossal squid was found in Antarctic waters. The example found was still immature, but had an overall length of around 50 feet. Octopi by comparison, are small fry, and the biggest, caught in March 2002, only measured 13 feet. So the beast at St. Augustine is still a truly unexplained phenomenon.

THE MONGOLIAN DEATHWORM

UNDER THE BURNING sand dunes of the Gobi desert there lurks a creature that is so feared by the Mongolian people they are scared even to speak its name. When they do, they call it the 'Allghoi khorkhoi,' which means 'the intestine worm,' because this fat, red, deadly snake-like monster looks similar to a cow's innards.

This giant worm, measuring up to four feet long, can kill people instantly. How it does it, no one knows. Some believe it spits a lethal toxin, others say it emits a massive electrical charge. However it kills, it does so quickly and can do it from a distance. We in the West have come to call this monster the 'Mongolian Deathworm.'

Artist's impression of a Mongol Death Worm, based on eyewitness reports.

Mongolian Nomads believe the giant worm covers its prey with an acidic substance that turns everything a corroded yellow colour. Legend says that as the creature begins to attack it raises half its body out of the sand and starts to inflate until it explodes, releasing the lethal poison all over the unfortunate victim. The poison is so venomous that the prey dies instantly.

Because Mongolia had been under Soviet control until 1990, very little was known about the Deathworm in the West. In recent years, investigators have been able to look for evidence of the creature's existence. Ivan Mackerle, one of the leading Loch Ness Monster detectives, studied the region and interviewed many Mongolian people about the worm. Due to the sheer volume of sightings and strange deaths, he came to the conclusion that the Deathworm was more than just legend.Nobody is entirely sure what the worm actually is. Experts are certain it is not a real worm because the Gobi desert is too hot an area for annelids to survive. Some have suggested it might be a skink, but they have little legs and scaly skin whereas witness accounts specify the worm is limb-less and smooth bodied. The most probable explanation is that it is a type of venomous snake. Although the native Mongolian people are convinced of the Deathworm's nature, it will take more years of research to satisfy the rest of the world's scientific community.

MOTHMAN

THIS STORY SOUNDS like the creation of an overworked comic book writer. A seven-foot-tall, well built, humanoid monster with giant red, glowing eyes and huge brown wings, a creature who can ascend to the skies from a standing position, and fly at astonishing speeds, and who mutilates pets and instils instant fear in the hearts of all those who see him. Yet, for over a year in the mid 1960s more than 100 otherwise reliable residents of a small West Virginian town distinctly saw the horrifying figure that terrorised their community. They saw 'Mothman.'

In early November 1966 various sightings of a huge, strange 'bird' were reported around Point Pleasant, West Virginia, USA. On 12th November, five gravediggers preparing a plot reported seeing a 'brown human being' take to the air from some nearby trees and pass over their heads. It was not until three days later that the creature really terrified the community with a close encounter.

What do you see?

On 15th November, two young couples were driving together near the McClintic Wildlife Preserve, just outside Point Pleasant. The area was known to locals as 'TNT,' because it had been used as an explosives depot during the Second World War and there were many abandoned chemical and industrial plants in the vicinity. Late in the evening, the two couples approached an old generator plant and saw that its door appeared to have been ripped off. It was then that they noticed two huge red eyes shining out of the gloom at them. These hypnotic, staring discs were attached to what they said was 'shaped like a man, but bigger, maybe six or seven feet tall. And it had big wings folded against its back.'

As the creature approached, the young group sped off, but as they looked back they saw it take to the air, rising straight up without flapping its wings. It had a giant 10-foot wingspan, and kept pace with the car despite the vehicle reaching speeds of 100 miles an hour. Eventually the group reached the Point Pleasant city limits, where their aerial pursuer turned away and disappeared. The couples drove straight to the local police station and reported what they had seen. Although local police found nothing at TNT, they accepted the young people had seen something.

Over the next few days reports of a giant 'bird' terrorising locals came into police headquarters with increasing frequency. Car passengers had experienced the creature swooping down on them, and the reception on television and radio sets were being disrupted across the region. One man whose television failed lived in Salom, 90 miles from Point Pleasant. At the exact moment his television stopped working, his dog whined from the porch. The man went outside to investigate and spotted two red, glowing lights in his hay barn, at which point his dog ran off. The man, stricken with fear, returned to his house, locked all the doors and windows. That night, he slept with his gun next to him. His dog was never seen again.

Perhaps the most chilling story concerning Mothman happened on 16th November 1966. A young mother was driving to see some friends, who had one of the few houses close to the TNT compound. She said she had seen a 'funny red light' in the sky, and, as she arrived at her friends' house, heard something rustling near her car.

'It seemed as though it had been lying down. It rose up slowly from the ground. A big grey thing. Bigger than a man, with terrible glowing eyes,'

she said. Horrified, she grabbed her small daughter and ran into the house, locking the doors behind her. The creature followed, creeping onto the porch and staring in the windows. The police were called, but by the time they arrived, Mothman had disappeared.

Over the next year, Mothman was seen by many witnesses including firemen and pilots. Gradually the reports altered into cases of UFOs, strange lights and 'Men in Black.' At 17.00 on 15th December 1967 the Silver Bridge linking Point Pleasant to Ohio suddenly collapsed, 46 people died as a result, and the residents of Point Pleasant were forced to deal with real horror rather than mythical beasts. Their creature's reign of terror paled into insignificance and he was forgotten. However, many people still believe the bridge disaster may have been Mothman's terrible final act.

THE OGOPOGO

WANTED CRIMINALS OFTEN have a reward attached to their heads. Now it seems mythical beasts are also the object of bounty hunters' affections. Between August 2000 and September 2001 three companies from around Lake Okanegan promised $2 million to anyone who could find definitive, living proof that the fabled Ogopogo monster did exist. The crime the creature committed is hard to say, although there are stories of it seizing and murdering helpless native people out on the lake. It cannot be denied that the Ogopogo is a serial offender at causing civil unrest.

Lake Okanegan is in British Columbia, Canada. It is around 100 miles long and has areas almost 1000 feet deep. The native Salish tribe believed in a terrible serpent, which they called 'N'ha-a-tik,' the 'Lake Demon.' They said the beast had a cave dwelling near the middle of the lake, and they would often make sacrifices to please the monster. European settlers initially scoffed at the legends, but over the years the Ogopogo has established itself in the minds of many who live nearby.

From the mid 1800s white immigrants started seeing strange phenomena in the lake. One of the first stories told of a man crossing the lake with his two tethered horses swimming behind. Some strange force pulled the animals under, and the man only saved himself by cutting the horses loose.

Witnesses say the creature is anything up to 50 feet long, with green skin, several humps and a huge horse-like head. Some people have managed to closely view it as it ate water vegetation; they said the Ogopogo also had small feet or fins. It could be the North American cousin of the Loch Ness Monster. Most sightings have come from around the city of Kelowna, near the centre of the lake, and many monster watchers now agree that it seems to live in the area originally indicated in native legend.

The Skunk Ape

In the mid 1970s, a few years after the public release of Bigfoot footage, Florida police received a torrent of reports claiming a similar creature was living in the state's swamplands. Many witnesses described the beast as like an ape standing upright, seven feet tall and covered in light brown hair. In all it sounded like a Bigfoot clone, but there was one unique aspect to the Florida monster – it smelled like a strong mixture of rotten eggs, manure and an elephant's cage. One witness said it had the scent of a skunk that had just been rolling around inside a dustbin lorry. It was given the name the 'Skunk Ape.'

After the initial flurry of sightings, the Skunk Ape phenomenon waned. Some pictures, footprint casts and hair samples were collected, but appearances of the Skunk Ape came to an abrupt halt. There were suggestions it had been caught by the US Army and imprisoned at the Everglades National Park. This urban myth said that the creature escaped by smashing through a concrete wall and returned to his swampland home. Some Skunk Ape watchers believe he has taken up residence at the Big Cypress National Preserve, but none of the 70 rangers who patrol the area have ever seen him.

In the last few years however, new sightings have appeared in Ochapee, Florida. A group of tourists who were being shown round the Everglades saw a large ape-like creature moving around the edge of a nearby swamp. Later it was seen crossing the road outside the house of a local fire chief. The man found his camera and photographed the beast as it retreated into the swampland.

Skunk ape, or nocturnal monkey? Only the creature in the photograph knows for sure!

The photo does show a large brown, hirsute monster, but even the man who took the photograph says he thinks the creature could well be a man in an ape-suit. With confidence like that from first-hand witnesses, what hope is there that the Skunk Ape really exists?

THE UTAH LAKES MONSTERS

UTAH FOLKLORE SAYS the state's Great Lakes house not one, not two, but five fearsome water monsters. Early Native Americans believed some lakes were cursed by 'Water Babies' who would coax travellers into the water to their deaths. By the time pilgrim settlers started to arrive, local tribes told tales of a giant water lizard, thirty feet long, with large ears and a mouth that would swallow men whole. Local natives said the great serpents had disappeared in the 1820s, but by the 1860s white settlers were reporting incidents involving huge, terrifying, scaly creatures.

The Utah and Bear Lakes in the north have had most sightings of these monsters; indeed, the description witnesses provide suggest these lakes each have one of a pair of twin water-dragons. One of the first appearances of these creatures was in 1864 when a local man, Henry Walker, was in the Utah Lake. He reported seeing something that looked like a giant snake, but with the head of a greyhound, which frightened him so much he fled the water. Over the years, there were frequent accounts of reputable people, including local priests, meeting the beasts. All witnesses provided the same description – that of a giant snake's body with short, trunk-like legs rising out of the water with an enormous mouth and fearsome black eyes.

In the late 1860s the idea of hunting down the monsters gained favour. Young local men tried shooting at them. Some successfully hit their targets, although no one was ever able to sufficiently wound the beasts in order to capture them. One farmer heard rustling in his garden one night. Using only his old rifle, he confronted and shot the creature, only to discover it was his neighbour's heifer. In 1870 real physical evidence was recovered, when fishermen from Springsville, a nearby town, found a large unidentified skull with a five-inch tusk on the jaw. The next year the Salt Lake Herald even revealed that the monster had been caught, but what happened to the body of the captured creature is unknown.

In 1871 two local men were out fishing on Bear Lake when they saw the monster rise from the water. They said they managed to hit the beast with shots from their rifles, but the beast just swam away. A wagon train captain called William Budge said in 1874 that he had also seen the Bear Lake beast. Budge reported that the creature had been about 20 yards from shore when it surfaced from the water. 'Its face and part of its head was covered with fur or short hair of a light snuff colour,' he said. Bridge also described it as having a flat face with large eyes, prominent ears and a four or five-feet-long neck.

Bear Lake residents were so affected by Bridge's testimony that they decided to make a trap to capture the beast. Two prominent local citizens, Brigham Young and Phineas Cook, hatched a plan which involved little more than a giant fishing line. They linked a 300-feet-long, one-inch-thick rope to a large hook with a huge slab of mutton attached as bait. The position of the rope was marked by a buoy floating on the lake surface. Although the trap was often robbed of meat, no monster was ever caught.

Lake monster sightings had fallen away drastically by the end of the nineteenth century. There was one sighting of the Utah Lake creature in 1921, which marked a limited resurgence in interest, but then the whole area once again quietened down. Since then, one of the few reliable reports was in 1946 by a local Scout master who said he had seen the bizarre creature appear on the surface of the lake. The account was widely regarded to be so detailed and accurate that only the most ardent sceptic could doubt it. Local wags have also pointed out that Scouts don't lie. But some still do question the truth of the Utah Lakes monsters. In his lecture on the subject to the Utah State Historical Society, local historian D. Robert Carter said he actually believed the monster was a species of giant bug – humbug.

THE WHITE RIVER MONSTER

O F ALL THE awesome and hideous mystery beasts in the world, nothing is loved by its neighbours quite as much as 'Whitey,' the White River Monster. In fact, Arkansas State Legislators have declared the area where it has been most often seen – around the town of Newport – a 'White River Monster Refuge'. It is now illegal to 'molest, kill, trample or harm' the legendary beast. But this has not always been the case – originally locals wanted to dynamite the monster.

Whitey's first appearance was in the 1890s. He then reappeared in 1915, but it was only in the first week of July 1937 that he really made a splash. Men fishing in the White River, a tributary of the great Mississippi, noticed that they were finding it hard to land many fish. One day they spotted a strange creature in an eddy, and reported it to the local plantation owner, Bramlett Bateman. Bateman was sceptical, but agreed to have a look at whatever they had found. He was shocked at what he saw. A monster with the skin of an elephant, four or five feet wide by twelve feet long, with the face of a catfish, was lolling on the surface of the water.

Bateman felt this beast was a threat to his crops, and applied to local officials to blow up the eddy with TNT. The authorities refused permission, and by then hundreds of people had heard of the phenomenon. They came from as far away as California, some with cameras, some with explosives; one man reportedly brought a machine gun. A plan to capture the monster with a giant net fell by the wayside, and Bateman's use of a deep-sea diver to find the creature came to nought. As people lost interest in the beast, Bateman felt he was being accused of creating a hoax although there had been over 100 confirmed sightings recorded during the short period of excitement.

Whitey was forgotten, but he made a

dramatic return in June 1971. A man was fishing with two friends when suddenly a great fountain of water spurted in front of them and a creature with a 20-feet-long spikey back was seen to surface and then disappear beneath the water. The man managed to take a photograph of the beast, which he sold to the Newport Daily Independent newspaper. People who saw the picture were unimpressed by its clarity and the newspaper has since lost the original copy.

However, numerous other witnesses saw a long, grey creature surfacing in the water of the White River. Some said it was the length of a boxcar, that its smooth flesh looked as if it was peeling. Others said it made a bizarre noise, like a cow's moo or horse's neigh. Those who managed to see the beast's face in detail told of a strange tusk protruding from its forehead. A trail of peculiar 14 inch tracks were found on the nearby Towhead Island, and a CBS news team was duly despatched to report on the area. The last reported

sighting came in late July when two people out fishing claimed their boat was rocked by what they believed was the monster. Media coverage killed off sightings of Whitey, and in February 1973 the Arkansas Senate passed its resolution to protect the beast.

From the accounts witnesses have provided, some experts believe Whitey may be a lost elephant seal. They can be immense creatures, up to twenty feet long, and the descriptions of noise, skin and forehead horn would all fit correctly. It is also known that the elephant seal migrates seven thousand miles each year so it may just be off-course. However, the nearest seal colony lies on the west coast of America, so it would have to come through the Panama Canal to reach the White River. Also, elephant seals only live for around fifteen years, so no one, single animal could account for sightings over almost a century. Whatever Whitey is, he can be assured of a warm, if not explosive, welcome the next time he pops up in Arkansas.

The White River Monster: scaring rednecks for a century.

YETI

I N 1921 LT. COLONEL Charles Kenneth Howard-Bury, a British soldier leading an expedition up Mount Everest, recounted a puzzling story. His team had been scaling the mountain's north face when they noticed dark shapes moving about in the snow above them. By the time the explorers reached the site, the only signs of life were large, unusual, human-like footprints. Howard-Bury said his Sherpa guides called this creature the 'Metoh-Kangmi.' Translated, this became the 'Abominable Snowman.'

In fact, 'Metoh-Kangmi' was a collective term for any of three mythical mountain creatures. Individually, they had their own names – the 'Dzu Teh,' a large, hairy beast which experts believe is actually one of the rare bear species in the region, 'Thelma,' which is regarded as being a species of gibbon, and the 'Meh-Teh' or 'Yeh-Teh,' the 'man-beast' or 'rock dweller.' This final animal is the most enigmatic. It is described as being between five and six feet tall, with reddish hair, long hanging arms, a conical, pointed head and a human face. This 'Yeh-Teh' is what we now know as the Yeti.

In 1925 a Greek photographer called N. A. Tombazi was on expedition in the Himalayas when one of his Sherpa guides pointed at a figure in the distance. Tombazi said the creature stood upright, just like a human, and was pulling at some rhododendron bushes. The beast disappeared before Tombazi could capture it on film, but the party headed over to the area where it had been viewed and found footprints strangely

Abominable; could this be the footprint of a Yeti?

similar to human feet. During the following years, there were many reports of odd tracks in the snow.

In 1951 the eminent mountaineers, Eric Shipton and Michael Ward, were part of the Everest Reconnaissance Expedition. They were trying to plot the best route up the mountain when they came upon a set of fresh, unusual footprints. Shipton and Ward took photographs of the 13 by 18-inch prints, and followed the trail before it eventually disappeared. Sir Edmund Hilary and Sherpa Tenzing Norgay, the two most celebrated visitors to Everest, actually found giant footprints on their way to the summit in 1953. This was particularly interesting because Norgay's father was supposed to have encountered a Yeti shortly before he died, whereas Hilary later lead an effort to find evidence of the Yeti's existence.

When Hilary's 1960 Yeti expedition found nothing, the great man stated that the beast was nothing more than a fairy tale. But many experts felt Hilary had rather rushed to his conclusions. Even Hilary's colleague on the mission, Desmond Doig, said the expedition had been too bulky and clumsy. Doig agreed that they had not encountered a Yeti, but neither had they seen a snow leopard, which undoubtedly exists.

This failed expedition killed off much interest in the Yeti, but over the years more unusual footprints were found. In 1974 one of the creatures reportedly attacked a Sherpa girl and her yaks, killing a couple of her animals. Then, in March 1986, Tony Woodbridge, a British physicist doing a sponsored solo run around the Himalayas, had a remarkable face-to-face meeting with the monster. Woodbridge had seen tracks earlier in the day, but thought no more about it until he heard a crashing sound like an avalanche.

Further up the trail, snow had indeed fallen, creating a giant impenetrable frozen wall. Strangely, it looked as if something had slid down the snow. Woodbridge followed prints at the bottom of the mound, and 150 metres away he spotted a large, hairy, powerfully built creature standing stock-still. The beast did not move an inch, and Woodbridge was lucky enough to have his

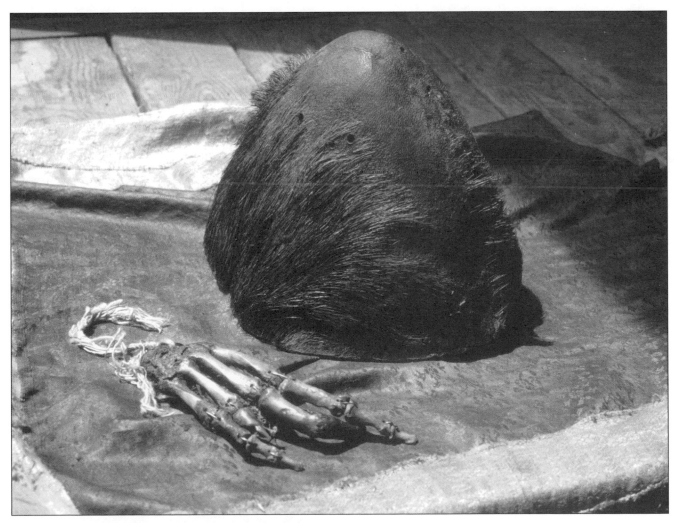

Skull top and skeletal hand, said to be from the Yeti.

21

camera on him. Unfortunately, despite Woodbridge's initial strong convictions, close examinations of his photographs instilled some doubt and a return to the area convinced Woodbridge that he had only encountered a tree stump.

Even if episodes like this do nothing to convince sceptics, many experts agree that the idea of an unknown species of ape is not so far-fetched. Some species of wild cattle and jungle deer have only been discovered in the last ten years. It is possible that Yeti-like creatures, descended from prehistoric apes could be roaming parts of the world completely undiscovered. Whatever the scientists and experts prove, Sherpas have already accepted the belief that up in their mountains they are not alone.

CONSPIRACIES
AND
COMMUNICATIONS

ABDUCTIONS

Little green man: a common view of what an alien 'should' look like.

BECAUSE ALIENS ARE supposed to blank the minds of their victims, what actually happens during an abduction is often only revealed through regressive hypnosis or piecing together known facts. However, the stories which occur all follow broadly similar lines. Generally, the abductor feels compelled, or is forced, to go into an alien space-craft where they encounter the visitors. These are often described as being small, grey figures with large black eyes and a hairless body. They are frequently reported as having large skulls and they communicate with their human captive using telepathy. The message sent to the man or woman tells them not to be scared, that they will not be harmed.

The candidate is scanned, or examined, and then placed on an operating table. This part of the abduction is often a blur, even during the hypnosis, but it seems the aliens perform a series of tests and a recurring theme is that they do extensive sexual experiments on their subject. The abductee's body is prodded, probed and manipulated. Some even report having tracking devices or other equipment implanted under their skin.

The human is returned to wherever they were picked up, often remembering absolutely nothing. Consequently they are left in a state of perplexion as they realise a number of unaccountable hours have passed. The physical effects are said to be striking. Many people are bruised all over their bodies, and suffer painful headaches the next morning. Abductees often have terrible nosebleeds and bizarre but small puncture wounds at points on their skin. They are also said to pass strange urine the next morning. Female abduction victims are particularly prone to suffering sexual pains. In all cases, an extreme sense of fatigue is felt.

The psychological results are often even more extreme. Some people feel as if they love the aliens and have been enriched by contact. These abductees believe the visitors have come to warn us and help Mankind protect the planet. But these types of experiences are in the minority. Many feel a sense of violation and despair, very similar to rape victims. Often it is mixed with confusion, disbelief and a sense of possible insanity. Many abduction victims need counselling to regain some sense of stability and, in cases of extreme trauma, have been known to commit suicide. However, many researchers wonder if abduction memories are themselves caused by psychological problems, rather than the reverse.

The first time alien abductions entered the public consciousness was in September 1961 when Barney and Betty Hill were reportedly captured by strange beings. The Hills gave an account under hypnosis a few years later that revealed all manner of strange experiments had been performed on them. Betty had seen the aliens inserted a probe into her belly button, and Barney claims he was forced to provide a sample of his sperm. The one incongruous detail they did provide was that the aliens, rather than having large black eyes, actually had 'wraparound' receptors. Sceptics point out that the Hills' testimonies were given less than a fortnight after a television episode about aliens with wraparound eyes.

This factor is one that repeatedly features in abduction stories. The descriptions of aliens and their craft are often identical to stereotypical, 1930s style cosmic invaders. No details have been revealed which could not have been derived from the imagination of a comic book writer. Similarly, no souvenirs have been brought back from the any craft visited by humans. However there are also a few examples featuring extremely disturbing physical evidence. One is where a pregnant woman was abducted by aliens who removed her foetus. Although she had previously gone for an ultrasound that had confirmed her unborn children was present and doing fine, when she went to the doctors afterwards, it had simply disappeared. The second example involves people who have actually found alien implants in their body. There is even a rumour that a private clinic in California has removed a number of strange implants from abductees' bodies. If these stories are true, there can be no denying that alien meetings leave physical scars on the victim.

The reported evidence on the bodies of abductees is hard to dismiss, and if an implant is ever officially removed and studied, it could act as conclusive proof. Until then, many scientists are going to be sceptical that this phenomenon is nothing more that the product of imaginations easily prone to fantasy.

ANCIENT ASTRONAUTS

ERICH VON DANIKEN'S book Chariots of the Gods has many followers who believe it is the most convincing text supporting the idea of alien travellers instigating Mankind's traditions. He claims that the first UFOs ever to visit the Earth landed in prehistoric times, and the aliens that alighted were really the beings responsible for our ancient ancestors' intelligence. Such a theory encompasses countless tales of ancient, now lost, races. The legends of Lemuria, Atlantis and Nazca all have elements that encourage intergalactic relation-ships, and Daniken's daring suggestions have spurned countless similar theories linking our history with visits from ancient astronauts.

Daniken was born on 14th April 1935 in

Zofingen, Switzerland. At school he was fascinated by ancient holy writings, but it was during his time managing a Swiss hotel that he wrote his first and most famous book, Chariots of the Gods. The book looked at evidence to support a theory that prehistoric Man did not have the abilities to create his own civilisations. Daniken stated that ancient astronauts had arrived on the planet and introduced our ancestors' culture, traditions and intelligence. By carefully choosing data from religious, historical, scientific, biological, mythical and even some downright fictional sources, Daniken created a compelling argument. But many other experts have since had to question his assertions.

He claimed that the Ark of the Covenant was made as a large electric capacitor, when in fact its design is utterly impractical. Famously, he stated that the fabled Nazca lines are runways for alien spacecraft, but did not consider the other options: for example, that they might have something to do with native Nazcan culture. He introduced impossible equations and even fictional 'facts.' One example of Daniken's evidence was pottery said to date from Biblical times. The ancient pots had pictures of UFOs painted in their sides, but a television documentary team found the potter who created the artefacts. When Daniken was confronted with proof of his fraud, he replied that it was allowed because some people will irrationally refuse to believe an argument unless they see tangible evidence.

Since then, rival or complementary theories about similar subjects have appeared. Another controversial notion was written by Robert Bauval and Adrian Gilbert in their 1994 book The Orion Mystery. The idea is termed 'The Orion Theory,' and is solely connected with the belief that the Ancient Egyptians are descended from alien visitors. Gilbert and Bauval realised that the three pyramids at Giza correlate exactly with the three belt stars of Orion. Subsequent study using the theory has apparently discovered other ancient structures in areas of Egypt that correspond to points of the Orion constellation.

The Orion Theory suggests that the alien visitors originated from a planet in the Orion constellation. The Egyptians worshipped the god Osiris, who had 'Sha' as its cosmic representation. The Sha constellation is what we call Orion. Gilbert and Bauval also studied the strange shafts found in the pyramids which they said were directed towards the right area of the heavens for the dead pharaohs' souls to ascend back from whence they came. Modern scholars have pointed out that the Earth's position and view of the heavens would have been drastically different in ancient history, and suspicious manipulation of time frames has been used to make sure some related theories are seen as plausible. In reality this has undermined the integrity of the whole subject.

The forefather of all these types of ideas, Daniken himself, has little reason to be bitter about other people's doubts. Chariots of the Gods became an instant bestseller in the United States and across the world. Since then, he has written nearly 30 books and sold 60 million copies of his work. He enjoys a life of travel, lecturing across the world and appearing on television programmes talking abut his theories. He is responsible for inspiring a major science-fiction television series entitled Chariots of the Gods, and in the summer of 2003 he opened his very own Mysteries of the World theme park. Perhaps the mystery in this story is nothing to do with aliens and ancient civilisations, but how one man created an enormous industry and following based on a theory with dubious foundations?

The Great Pyramid of Giza: sophisticated map of the heavens, or just a load of stones?

Area 51

Deep in the Nevada desert lies a military base that is surrounded by so much official secrecy that the US government has even refused to acknowledge it exists. The base was built by the CIA and all pilots, ground crews and the staff have to retire from their original military departments and join the agency before taking residency on site. As a CIA installation it operates independently of other government departments. To this day, signs at the entrance warn all visitors that they have no constitutional rights on site, and rapid armed units guard the perimeter. It is the UFO world's worst kept secret, and the area is now a pilgrimage point for alien watchers. This is Area 51.

Built in the 1950s around the Groom Lake Air Force base, and next to the Nevada atomic test range, Area 51 was a perfect site to carry out classified aircraft tests. It had a large flat surface perfect for laying runways, few local residents, and a highly unattractive reputation to new settlers due to the nearby nuclear pollution. Initially it was built purely for testing the U2 spy plane, but the programme was such a success that all the United States secret aircraft were experimentally flown there. The base grew in size, creating its own small community and the landing strip was increased to three miles long. The Blackbird and Stealth planes were developed on site, and countless unknown technologies are housed in the base's hanger. Many people believe these technologies are, quite literally, from a different planet, and the base is actually a test zone and hiding site for alien aircraft. At night, strange lights

Examining the wreckage of a UFO – or is it a weather balloon?

are seen in the sky above the base, and many watchers believe the site hides enormous underground installations.

More in-depth knowledge of operations there have come through one man, Bob Lazar. Lazar is a scientist who was employed by a company called E G & G in 1989 who said they were working on a propulsion project at their testing centre near Area 51, on a base called S4. In later conversations Lazar revealed that he and other scientists were employed to pull an alien aircraft apart and see if they could manufacture it using man-made components. As part of their work, the scientists were given information about the role of aliens in the history of the Earth, and on one occasion Lazar even claims to have briefly seen, first-hand, a real, live alien at S4.

Over time, Lazar says he decided to rebel against his employers. In the evening of 22nd March 1989 he and a friend went out to the Groom Lake road and watched a flying disc test flight. The following week Lazar, his friend and three others visited the same area. They saw a disc flight, which Huff described as 'the thrill of a lifetime.' The disc they witnessed glowed extremely brightly, and flew so close that they felt they had to move backwards. The following week, on the way back home from another UFO-spotting trip, the group were seen and stopped by base security patrolling the outlying area. The next day Lazar was sacked from EG & G's employment. He has subsequently revealed that nine discs are said to be held at S4.

Some of the unsettling things that go on at the base are more real than others. The road to its entrance is known as 'The Widow's Highway' because of the high numbers of

workers at the base who die through contact with fatally poisonous materials. Many experts suggest the area is a secret dumping ground for toxic substances, rather than a UFO base. In either case, the workers are sworn to secrecy, and cannot reveal details about what they have been handling to their doctors. This has lead to their wives launching court proceedings against the US government, who have traditionally refuted the allegations on the grounds that Area 51 does not officially exist. However, a statement made in January 2001 by President George Bush did refer to the 'operating location near Groom Lake,' which is the first official recognition of Area 51. But Bush also said that the site was exempt from environmental disclosure requirements, so the widows are still fighting their case. But at least we now know the place is not just a figment of our imaginations.

CIVILIAN AIRCRAFT ENCOUNTERS

ONE OF THE FIRST ENCOUNTERS between a civilian aircraft and a UFO happened at 2.45am on 24th July 1948. Captain Clarence S. Chiles and Pilot John B. Whitted, both former US Air Force pilots, were flying an Eastern Airlines DC-3 flight from Atlanta, Georgia to Montgomery, Alabama. The plane was travelling at an altitude of 5,000 feet when both men noticed a strange aerial vehicle approaching their aircraft. They said it appeared to be cigar-shaped, 400 foot long, and travelled at around 600 miles an hour. They managed to make out two rows of windows along its side, which glowed bright white, and a blue light underneath. It had no wings and its trail rocked the DC-3 as it blasted off. For the rest of the 1940s and 1950s many aeroplanes were 'buzzed' by UFOs, and the phenomenon grew to such an extent that military officials brought in a code that gagged US commercial pilots from talking about their experiences.

On the other side of the border, in Canada, pilots did not have to follow such regulations. In 1966 a Canadian Pacific DC-8 was flying at a height of 35,000 feet from Peru to Mexico City when the crew witnessed something very odd. The Captain, Roger Millbank, was so certain of what he and his staff had seen that he filed an official report with Mexican authorities. He said that he and the co-pilot had seen two bright white lights to the left, which gradually separated and approached the DC-8. The lights seemed to change in colour and intensity, and they turned into two distinct beams, pointing in a V-shape. They came nearer still, and finally levelled off by the airliner's left wing-tip. Millbank said that in the light of the full moon they could 'see a shape between the two lights, a structure which appeared to have been thicker in the middle.' It remained close to the DC-8 for a couple more minutes, and then disappeared behind.

On one flight in the 1970s the passengers on a British Airways jet had a very light-hearted encounter with a UFO. The plane was flying just south of the Portuguese capital, Lisbon, when the Captain heard air traffic control issuing a warning about a strange object in the skies near their flight-path. The crew of the BA flight saw a bright light in the distance, and a cigar-shaped craft soon appeared close-by. Realising this was too good an opportunity to miss, the British pilot issued an announcement over the passenger address system, 'Ladies and gentlemen, if you look on the starboard side of the plane, you will see what we believe to be a UFO.' The airliner reached its destination safely.

In November 1979, a rather more unpleasant episode befell the pilot flying a Spanish charter plane from Ibiza to the Spanish mainland. At an altitude of 24,000 feet a strange subject almost collided with the airliner. The pilot saw a bright red object, seemingly on a collision course with his vessel, and began an emergency dive to avoid it. The UFO continued to buzz round the airliner, and in the end two fighter jets were sent to intercept the object. The whole incident was witnessed on radar screens and by countless people watching from the earth below. A similar occurrence happened in the same area exactly one year later. The pilot of an Iberian Airways jet flying at 31,000 feet suddenly saw an immense green bubble in his flight-path. The phenomenon was witnessed by six other commercial airlines in the vicinity, and some reports said it even swooped down on Barcelona Airport.

In recent years, other similar incidents have occurred. A British Airways 737 was arriving at Manchester Airport in 1995 when a UFO buzzed near to the side of the plane. An even closer event happened on 12th June 1998 when an Oslo-bound jet took off from London's Heathrow Airport. The plane's captain reported to air traffic controllers that they had almost been hit by a small aircraft. Later the co-pilot said he had seen a very clear bright light and the captain filed an official report claiming a fighter-sized aeroplane had passed within a 50 metre distance of the aircraft. Aviation, military and police authorities found no explanation for the incident, however they say that no matter how safe air travel is, accidents sometimes do happen. With this level of unexplained aerial activity, perhaps it's surprising they do not occur more often.

GOVERNMENT KNOWLEDGE

IN DECEMBER 1988 countless witnesses in Puerto Rico saw apparent encounters between US warplanes and strange, huge alien aircraft. On one occasion, bystanders saw two F-14 jets actually enter another massive flying triangular craft. Were the war planes destroyed or were they co-operating in joint manoeuvres with the unknown vessel? Certainly some conspiracy theorists have suggested that the United States government actually has a close relationship with alien visitors, and provides them with ground bases. One of the areas is said to be under the water of the western Atlantic. Other theories propose that extraterrestrial beings are allegedly abducting law abiding US citizens in return for technological secrets. But what do our governments really know about UFOs?

The US Department of Defense does not, officially, have anything to do with UFOs anymore. That is because they no longer call the UFOs. In the present age, such phenomenon are called Uncorrelated Targets, or UCTs for earthbound unidentified air-based incidents. The US military rarely reveals what it knows, and exact figures are scarce. Officially there is also no central department dealing with the issue, although many investigators consider this to be a fallacy. In either case, this situation has only developed since 1974 with the shutting down of the US military's open, public examination of UFO cases.

After the Second World War, a spate of UFO sightings initiated a US project called 'Operation Blue Book.' It was a scheme designed to show the public there was no secrets in the US's official investigation of alien craft. This 'openness' was merely a front, and it was actually made a crime equal to spying for military officers to reveal details of UFOs to unauthorised people. In reality, Blue Book only reported cases that were guaranteed to be found as hoaxes or mistaken identity. One of the experts who worked as a scientific consultant on the project was Josef Allan Hynek, an astrophysicist and sceptic. He revealed that any sightings reported by people under 18 years of age were automatically ignored, and other incidents would only be published if they could be rationalised. In total, Blue Book investigated 15,000 reports of UFOs, many of them still not explained, and Hynek himself experienced something of a conversion. He became an informed believer, and coined the term 'close encounter.'

Britain has its own group of people similar to Hynek. Nick Pope was a civil servant who worked for the Ministry of Defence. His role was to respond to questions from the public about UFOs. During the course of his work, he uncovered enough fascinating information to write his own books about unexplained phenomenon. Other investigators believe what Pope has been privy too is merely the tip of the iceberg, and some

quite extraordinary files concerning the issue of UFOs have been uncovered. One collection entitled 'UFO Policy' features a six-page document from 1960 which states that any unauthorised information disclosures would be viewed as breaches of the Official Secrets Act.

The Ministry of Defence official policy states that it does not investigate UFO sightings unless they are of 'defence significance.' Despite impressive proof or terrifying witness accounts, the authorities at the Ministry of Defence continually rule that each incident has no importance to national security. At least that is the public position, and what happens behind the scenes is unknown.

One of the problems British investigators have when searching for old files like this is that the various ministries and departments involved are quite adept at being secretive. United States officials, on the other hand, are supposed to be more open. The American Constitution and Freedom of Information Act is designed to let the public know what is actually happening. In 1980, however, a group called 'Citizens Against Unidentified Flying Objects Secrecy' sued the National Security Agency. It wanted the NSA to open its files on 239 UFO incidents but the authorities argued that to do so would damage US national safety. In recent years a ruling changing the classification status of documents has meant many of these reports will finally be put in the public domain.

One cannot help but feel that any truly amazing official papers that may cause public hysteria will be suppressed. Are national governments hiding the truth from their people, or is there really nothing to report? It is a question we may never definitely know.

LIFE ON MARS

THE IDEA THAT the Earth could be invaded by a marauding army of creatures from Mars is a scene now suitable only in vintage science-fiction – with the advent of modern technology and eater understanding, even our creative writers have progressed. The suggestion that intelligent life forms live so close to Earth is now too implausible for fiction. But as we learn more about the universe, so our intelligence contradicts old, established beliefs. Can it be true that conventional wisdom is wrong?

In 1976, Viking Orbiter 1 was sent to scan the surface of Mars. The craft was designed to photograph the planet's terrain and find a suitable landing site for a future Viking Landing 2 mission. Investigators studying the photographs found a picture of Mars' Cydonia region that seemed to show a mile-wide hill shaped like a human face. NASA claimed it was just a trick of the light, and released the image, naming it the 'Mars Face.' However, many enthusiasts believed that close scrutiny of the photographs proved that some formations were artificial, rather than naturally created. Some people stated that the face was the design of an intelligent life form, and some believed that triangular-shaped hills near the face were actually pyramids.

In 1998 and 2001 the Mars Global Surveyor took more photographs of the Cydonia region. These pictures showed the 'Mars Face' and other geographical objects as being much more innocent. However, most astonishingly, 'Mars Face' enthusiasts claimed these new pictures depicted a whole city frozen underneath a giant glacier in the region. NASA has promised to continue mapping the area until the question is answered and former NASA administrator, Dan Goldin, vowed that the Cydonia region of Mars will be studied to everybody's satisfaction.

Other developments in the quest to find life on Mars have also thrown up some fascinating results. A meteorite from Mars was found in Antarctica in 1984 and the NASA scientists who studied it found it contained evidence that bacterial life may actually exist, or have existed, on the planet. The space rock contained hydrocarbons, which are the natural waste products of dead micro-organism; mineral structures consistent with bacterial activity and tiny globules of carbonate, which may be micro-fossils. In NASA's opinion, these features found together strongly point to possible micro-organism activity.

Another recent discovery was published when data found by the Pathfinder mission to Mars suggested there might be chlorophyll in its soil. Pathfinder touched down in the Ares Vallis region of the planet in July 1997, and took many pictures and readings from the area in which it landed. Some of the pictures it took revealed two areas close to the landing site may have contained chlorophyll. Chlorophyll is a substance used by plants and other organisms to extract energy from sunlight. It is an important component of life on our planet, a very stark indicator that there may be life on another planet too.

The most important ingredient for life is

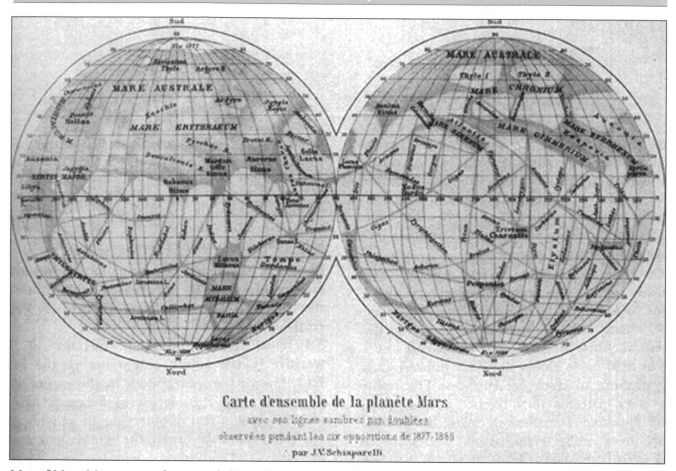

Carte d'ensemble de la planète Mars
avec ses lignes sombres non doublées
observées pendant les six oppositions de 1877-1888
par J.V. Schiaparelli.

Map of Mars. Many geographers now believe that the topography of the planet suggests that water may once have been present.

water. It had generally been assumed that there was little easily available water on the surface of Mars, and most of that was frozen solid. However, recent studies have suggested that the surface is actually just a covering over a permafrost layer. NASA and Russian scientists have looked at the examples of life found in permafrost regions of Earth, and believe similar organisms may lurk somewhere on Mars. Other experts who have studied the surface of the planet have noted how similar it is to former, now dried-up, river, lake and ocean areas on Earth. It all suggests that water was in abundance at some time on Mars.

American President George Bush certainly seems to share in this opinion, and his budget announcements have all favoured putting some money into space research, particularly on Mars. One statement said that 'habitable worlds' may be more prevalent than scientists once thought. He vowed to put $3 billion into Project Prometheus, a plan to find out more about our solar system. This money should prove to be highly beneficial for the Mars projects, for, as each new study seems to throw up more potential questions, it may well take nothing less than a manned mission to Mars to finally put the mystery to rest.

MEN IN BLACK

THE FIRST KNOWN ENCOUNTER with two 'Men in Black' happened in 1947. Two US harbour patrolmen, Harold A. Dahl and Fred L. Crisman, had spotted a UFO over the water of Puget Sound, Washington. Dahl said that a man dressed in black visited him shortly after the sighting and forcefully advised him not to discuss the incident further. A similar meeting happened to Carlo Rossi, from the area near San Pietro a Vico in Italy. In the early hours of 25th July, 1952, Rossi was fishing in the River Serchio when he witnessed a strange circular craft hovering over the river. Rossi hid, watching the craft as it passed over him, and then sped away. In the following weeks he told no-one about what he had seen, but on 15th September he found a stranger dressed in a dark blue suit waiting for him by the river. The stranger spoke Italian, but with an odd Scandinavian accent, and had very strange facial features. The man forcefully asked Rossi about what he had seen, but Rossi denied everything.

A bizarre Men in Black case happened on 18th May 1968, when UFO witnesses started contacting researchers. George Smyth was one of those who had seen a strange object in the skies above Elizabeth, New Jersey, USA. He began to receive visits from strange men, and received phone calls warning him not to attend upcoming UFO conventions or speak to independent investigators. A bizarre aspect of this case was that the three visitors Smyth described were apparently the men he had been told to avoid – the UFO enthusiasts John Keel, Gray Barker and James Moseley. What made this even more odd was that these three men were actually miles away from Smyth's house at the time of the visits.

Other UFO investigators in the area, John Robinson and his wife Mary, also noticed strange things happening to them. A large dark car seemed to be parked outside their house in New Jersey City, with a strange man inside constantly watching them. One day Mary went out and noticed their friend James Moseley making a spectacle of himself further up the street. She thought this was very strange, but went inside to make a drink for him, thinking he was there to visit them. But then the phone rang. To her surprise it was Moseley, not on a street corner in New Jersey City, but at his home in Manhattan.

In recent years, more incidents have been reported. On 15th January 1997 William Shearer experienced a UFO encounter in Essex, southern England. Four days later he had a knock at the door and outside stood two strange men, dressed in dark grey suits and long coats. One man stood on guard by a large imposing saloon car, the other stood at Shearer's threshold. This man was said to be very tall, deathly pale but with bright red lips, and spoke in a very unusual, almost automated, way. He repeatedly asked to come in but Shearer refused and the men finally said they would come back later.

A month later, Shearer was at work when two men appeared. One was the visitor who had stood by the car at the housecall, the other was a different man. They were both dressed in suits with hats, and they told him they wanted to talk about his UFO experience. They gave him exact details of the incident, details that Shearer felt only he should know, and were forceful in their

Men in Black: Will Smith and Tommy Lee Jones prepare to save the Earth in a still from the film of the same name.

requests. Shearer asked to see their ID, but the men just kept repeating a formulaic set of questions. In the end, Shearer refused to let them into his place of work and the two men disappeared. However, since then, he has reported blatant tapping activity when using his telephone.

Although no one can be absolutely certain, one theory is that these strange visitors are UFO investigators who belong to a research group that has standardised their visiting uniform. Others say they are actually aliens trying to cover their tracks. Sceptics believe they are pranksters or simply figments of witness's imaginations. In most cases, they claim to be from the CIA or intelligence agencies, and there is a theory that these organisations have been happy to assume such identities in recent years as a ready-made method of intimidation. The other option is, of course, that they are from a secret department of government intelligence, trying to control UFO and alien-related sightings.

NAZCA LINES

IN THE 1930S, when air travel was gaining popularity as the easiest way to cross the high altitude peaks of South America, passengers flying over the lofty plains of Peru, were greeted with quite a sight. Down on the arid, dry plateau of the Nazca desert, which is about 250 miles south of Lima and covers an area of approximately 200 square miles, was a plethora of massive markings, many in the shape of people and animals, although there were also hundreds of criss-crossing, randomly spaced lines. Locals had always known of the strange marks found on the dusty floor, although it was only now, from the air, that their true designs were revealed. The discovery sparked an interest and a study that continues to this day: people wanted to know why they were there, and what they meant.

The pictures themselves were created using the gravel, soil and distinctly coloured undercrust. Because the area experiences less than an inch of rainfall each year, and the effect of the wind on the surface is minimal, the shapes have been preserved over centuries. There are over 100 outlines of

Tracing the outline of the Nazca designs, properly viewable only from the air.

animals and plants, including a monkey, spider, hummingbird and even, it is thought, a spaceman. Countless straight lines form squares, triangles, trapezoids and all manner of strange angles. They seem to run in random directions and to random lengths – one even stretches for nine miles along the desert floor.

Over 3,000 years ago the area was inhabited by a race called the Nazca who had developed proficient techniques in pottery, weaving and architecture. They created highly effective irrigation systems and successfully grew crops in a harsh environment. It is widely believed that these people were responsible for drawing the lines, although the actual date of the lines' creation is impossible to determine. A nearby city called Cahauchi, just south of the lines, was recently discovered as being the probable home of the Nazcan line drawers. Experts were able to deduce that the majority of Nazcan people fled the city after a series of natural disasters, with the few native people who remained being exiled or killed by Spanish conquistadors.

But why would a race want to draw pictures that could only be appreciated from the sky? Perhaps the most celebrated theory was the one advanced by Dr Maria Reiche. She tried to prove that the lines correlated to important stars rising in the heavens, and the symbols of animals were actually native representations of star constellations. But her views were not universally supported due to the very fact that the lines cannot be dated. As the Earth's relationship with the universe turns, any line in any direction will correspond to some astronomical feature at some date. After a lifetime of study and fascination, Reiche died and was buried in the Nazca valley in 1998.

During the 1960s, writers such as Louis Pauwels, Jacques Bergier, and Erich von Daniken famously promoted ideas that the lines were runways or landing strip for alien visitors. Other theories suggest they are an astronomical calendar; that they were used for religious ceremonies; or that they indicated underground sources of water. One expert believes that, before the invention of weaving tools, the lines had men standing along them holding thread, in a version of a giant human loom. But exactly why the images were designed to be viewed from the air has never really been addressed. One quite astonishing theory is that the Nazca people were the original human aviators, and had developed the first rudimentary hot air balloon.

Our understanding of the Nazcan culture has developed with archaeological discoveries, but today the fate of the lines is in serious jeopardy. In recent years, political and advertising agencies have graffitied slogans on the patterns, whilst a recent surge in gold and copper mining in the area is defacing the designs with industrial activities and heavy traffic movements. The expanding local population needs a higher level of basic amenities, which has meant utility providers are now running cables and pipes over the site. Combined with the effects of natural weathering, this means that the most enigmatic and mysterious visual display of an ancient race is under threat of being lost from Man's history forever.

PIRI REIS MAP

IN 1929 A GROUP of historians at the Topkapi Palace in Istanbul, Turkey, found something rather fascinating. Imprinted on an old Gazelle skin dated 1513 they uncovered a segment of an amazing map. The chart seemed to depict part of the Atlantic Ocean and included the Americas and Antarctica in perfect detail. The mysterious thing was it had been drawn up only a few years after Columbus' discovery, and three centuries before Antarctica was even known about. Over the years since the find, debate has raged about how the cartographer had assimilated his knowledge. Did an advanced ancient race, or aliens, create his source charts, or have the map's features been adapted to fit wishful-thinking theories?

The map came to be named after its creator – Piri Reis. The word 'Reis' actually means 'Admiral,' and it was discovered that Muhiddin Piri had originally worked as a privateer for the Ottoman-Turkish empire, before accepting a role in the imperial navy. On his travels he had collected all manner of charts, sketches, drawings and diagrams of coastlines and lands in the known world. In 1513, using an exhaustive list of source charts and data, he drew his first world map, which is what we now recognise as the Piri Reis Map. He is known to have compiled another, quite different, global study in 1528 and continued to enjoy a distinguished military career until 1554, aged almost 90, when he was beheaded by the Ottoman Sultan.

The segment of the map that still exists is only a portion of the original, and shows the Atlantic Ocean from the west coast of Africa, to the east coast of South America, to the north coast of Antarctica in the south. Piri also included details about his sources on the map, claiming some of the reference charts he used were from the fourth century or even before. The map is not drawn with the straight lines of longitude and latitude found on today's maps. It was designed using a series of circles with lines radiating out from them. These types of charts were called 'portolan' maps and were used to explain sailing routes, guiding ships from port to port, rather than giving sailors a definite position in the world. Ancient charts of this type were widespread, and Columbus is said to have used one when he set off to find the Americas.

Many Piri Reis Map enthusiasts believe the level of geographical detail and mathematical knowledge needed to create the map was far beyond the reach of navigators from the sixteenth or earlier centuries. Indeed, experts at the United States Air Force in the 1960s found the map so accurate they used it to replace false information on their own charts. Some people believe the map could only have been achieved with the help of aerial surveys, and suggest alien creatures mapped the planet thousands of years ago, leaving their results behind to be copied by Mankind.

The map's seemingly accurate depiction of the geography of Antarctica is its most fascinating aspect. Antarctica was discovered in 1818, and the actual land of the continent was only mapped in 1949 by a combined British and Scandinavian project that had to use modern equipment to see the land underneath the mile-deep icecap. The theory put forward to compensate for this is that an ancient race using advanced, but now lost, technology were able to accurately record details of the continent before it was covered with ice.

Some experts suggest Antarctica was ice-free no later than 6,000 years ago, although others believe ice has covered the continent for – at least – hundreds of thousand of years. Similarly, many cartography experts claim the portolan system of map drawing now leaves its accuracy rather in the eye of the beholder, and many maps of this time included imaginary continents in the south Atlantic. But there are still some unexplainably accurate details on the map. The Falkland Islands are placed at the correct latitude, despite not being discovered until 1592, and the unknown Andes mountain range was included on the map of America. Similarly, Greenland was shown as three separate islands, a fact only discovered this century.

So the debate continues. Did Piri Reis just strike lucky with cartographic guesswork? Or did the Turkish admiral have access to charts and maps created by an advanced race, living on the planet thousands of years ago?

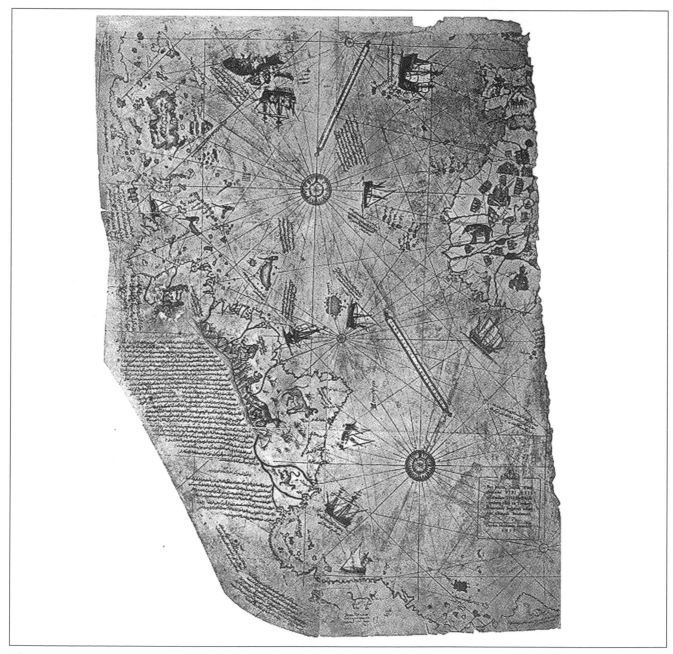

The Piri Reis map, showing the coastline of Antarctica *under the ice*.

RENDLESHAM FOREST

MANY AREAS ON THE east coast of Britain contain top-secret military installations. One island called Orford Ness, just off the coast of Suffolk, was the site of many still unrevealed chemical, biological, nuclear and radiological weapons experiments during the 1940s, 50s and 60s – and as a matter of interest has an imposing lighthouse. Some of the other bases near the coast have been leased to the US Air Force; the twin installations at RAF Bentwaters and RAF Woodbridge were two oval complexes and formed a vital part of NATO's defence against Communist threats. It was reported that at the height of the Cold War these co-joined airbases housed the most nuclear weapons outside the Soviet Union. This important and serious tactical presence meant the bases were fiercely guarded and woro hiddon in a thick ring of woodland known as Rendlesham Forest. In December 1980, two strange events, which were witnessed by some of the forces stationed at the bases, occurred in this forest and would go down in history as one of the most fascinating UFO cases ever recorded.

The unique aspect about the Rendlesham forest incident is that within three years of it happening, the public had proof of official, military documents detailing the events that were witnessed. The witnesses were not simple country folk, lunatics or publicity-seekers, they were trained, professional US Air Force personnel. Indeed, the most famous name connected with the incident, Lieutenant Colonel Charles Halt, was the Deputy Base Commander in charge of Bentwaters and Bridewater's security. Not only did Halt write and submit the official report, he was also a first-hand witness at the second of the two strange happenings.

His memo, sent to the British Ministry of Defence, was released by the US authorities under the American Freedom of Information Act in 1983, after rumours about a period of bizarre incidents at the site begun to circulate among UFO enthusiasts. The subsequent publication of sensational stories about Rendlesham appeared in tabloid newspapers, and the continued silence by British authorities meant many believed something odd did occur. So what did happen around the Rendlesham Forest in December 1980?

Halt's memo recorded that the first incident happened in the early hours of 27th December 1980. He wrote that two perimeter security patrolmen saw a strange light outside the back gate of RAF Woodbridge, which they thought may have been a crashed aircraft. They called their commanders for permission to investigate, and three patrol-men went to search the nearby land on foot. These three military guards reported viewing a bizarre glowing subject in the forest which appeared to be made of a metallic substance. It was triangular in shape, two to three meters wide and about two meters high. It was said to light the whole forest with a bright white beam. It had a red light as its peak, blue lights along its base, and seemed to hover or stand on legs. As the Air Force personnel approached it, the object weaved through the trees and disappeared, causing the nearby farm animals to go into a frenzy An hour later, the strange object was briefly seen again.

The next day, Halt wrote that more servicemen from the base ventured into the forest to see if they could see any markings or tracks. They found three, one-and-a-half-inch-deep and seven-inch-wide depressions in the area where the object was seen. On 29th December, base personnel tested for radiation levels and found higher-than-normal readings in the centre of the formation of depressions, and on a nearby tree.

During the night of the 29th, and the morning of the 30th, another 'red sun-like' light was viewed moving and pulsing in the forest. Halt personally saw the oddities and his memo reported that it 'appeared to throw off glowing particles and then broke into five separate white objects and then disappeared.' Three strange star-like objects were seen darting rapidly about the night sky exuding red, green and blue light. They remained visible for two to three hours, and 'beamed down a stream of light from time to time.'

Over time, many of the Air Force witnesses have come forward and offered their own accounts of what happened those nights. Halt himself took an audio, micro-cassette recording of his commentary as events happened on the second occasion. However, his official report was not written until 13th January 1981 and there now seems to be confusion with dates. Local police records show that they were called by the US Air Force about the first incident on the morning of 26th December 1980. On the other hand, some reports state that a nearby radar station at RAF Watton recorded an unusual 'uncorrelated target' that disappeared near Rendlesham Forest at around 2am on 27th December. Other researchers have revealed that Halt actually called RAF Watton in

relation to the second sighting at 3:25am on 28th December. Seemingly, there is a fundamental disagreement between Halt's dates of occurrences during the mornings of the 27th and 29th, and other agencies involved which state they happened early on the 26th and 28th.

Many investigators believe the events themselves were nothing more than the result of misunderstandings and visual illusions. The initial cause of the supposed UFO sighting may have been an exceptionally bright meteor that appeared over southern England just before 3am on 26th December. It has been suggested that the subsequent triangular, metallic object was in fact a tractor, seen from a distance with its night lights switched on. Many investigators believe the bizarre beam of white light see illuminating the forest was actually caused by the Orford Ness lighthouse. Similarly, there are benign explanations for the resulting depressions – they may have been indentation caused by old rabbit burrows. The radiation levels recorded, although higher than naturally expected, are said by some experts to be negligible.

It is undoubted that many of the US servicemen viewing these bizarre occurrences must have been extremely excited, and may have become confused and irrational. Certainly the police who visited the scene recorded no sighting of UFOs. However, the personnel were also trained airmen, and the bases at Bentwaters and Woodbridge had been occupied by US forces for many years, so they had grown accustomed to the area. The fact that these installations were the base for seriously powerful weapons meant that the staff there could not be prone to flights of fancy. Similarly, Woodbridge was the home of 67th Aeroplane Rescue and Recovery Squadron – a unit specialising in the retrieval of returning satellites and spacecraft. This highly advanced and technological group answers directly to the Pentagon in Washington, and one would hope they would have been able to identify the differences between any known aerial or space vehicle, and a tractor.

In recent years, the British Government silence – which lead many to believe in a UFO cover-up at Rendlesham – has receded. In fact, the complete file of documents relating to the incidents has been released. The official explanation that the Ministry of Defence had nothing to say on the matter because there 'was no reason to consider that the alleged sightings had any defence significance,' has been proven honest. The newly

publicised documents show the MOD did investigate the sightings but could find little evidence to cause the alarm.

Their analysis does not entirely coincide with the views of Georgina Bruni who wrote the seminal book on the Rendlesham UFO mystery, You Can't Tell the People. Bruni interviewed all available witnesses and was even given a personal tour around the US installations. She also managed to catch a quick unexpected word with the ultimate Chief of British forces at the time, the Prime Minister Margaret Thatcher. Her words to Bruni were interesting and mysterious,

'You must have the facts, and you can't tell the people.'

ROSWELL

THROUGH THE HAZY black and white footage, the relaxed shape of a bloated, swollen-headed, six-fingered humanoid figure can just be viewed. The grainy scene is a bizarre image of death as the pathologist cuts into the alien skin. Could this be the most incredible evidence ever uncovered to prove that something out of this world really did land at Roswell over fifty years ago?

On 7th July 1947 the wreckage of a strange vehicle and some non-human bodies was found on the Foster ranch just outside Roswell. The next day, a press officer from the Roswell Army Air Fields was happy to announce to the Roswell Daily Record that the 509th Bomb Group, an elite section of the Air Force, had salvaged an alien vessel. Immediately his words were refuted. The US 8th Air Force's commanding officer, General Roger Ramey, said they had actually recovered an experimental balloon. Ramey's explanation was quickly adopted as the

official line throughout the following years, and this technique of abject denial would continue to be championed by governments questioned about flying saucer stories.

Although the public initially accepted the official version of events, this episode sparked a consistent stream of UFO sightings, particularly around remote US Air Force bases. Sites such as Area 51 in Nevada, and the government's denial of its existence, led to suspicion and conspiracy theories. The 1947 'Roswell Incident' itself has also never quite left the public consciousness. In 1994 a New Mexico congressman instigated an inquiry into the affair. The investigative department of the US Congress, known as the General Accounting Office, discovered that many relevant US Air Force documents had gone missing or had been destroyed. However, the GAO also came to the conclusion that it was, indeed, a weather balloon that had been recovered from the Foster ranch, and the bodies there were in

The Roswell crash scene; why was there no debris left after the crash?

fact anthropomorphic dummies. Case closed.

Little did US officials realise that the 'Roswell Incident' was about to dramatically appear on television screens across the globe. In 1992, a British media businessman, Ray Santilli was in Cleveland, Ohio to meet a retired cameraman. Santilli wanted to buy some vintage 1955 Elvis footage from the man, who revealed he also had some interesting alien autopsy film from his time in the military. Santilli purchased the film in November 1994 and agreed to show it at the British UFO Research Association annual conference on 19th August 1995. However, by March 1995 news of the film had been released to the media, and a serious world premier of the footage was needed. It took place in front of invited guests at the Museum of London on 5th May. By the end of August 1995, millions of people around the world had seen moving pictures from a supposed alien autopsy.

Although this was compelling evidence, doubters immediately began voicing their theories about the film. The most obvious suspicion was that the autopsy had been created by movie special effects processes. Many experts believe the film is fake, but they also believe it is very high quality. The Hollywood effects industry is a closed shop, with insiders having friends and contacts across the range of companies, but so far no-one has an inkling as to who created the Roswell film. Other experts in the field of biology are less convinced that the body is entirely man-made, and some suspect that it may be a human being adapted to look other-worldly.

There is a whole host of further questions about the Roswell autopsy. Whoever captured the footage has never been revealed, although a bizarre film was released where someone purporting to be the cameraman attempted to explain his involvement. Santilli has never uncovered the footage he has of another alien autopsy and has never really allowed any of his films to be subjected to proper scrutiny. Most importantly, the aliens in the footage look nothing like the bodies witnesses saw recovered from the New Mexico desert floor. All experts who view the autopsy film agree that it is a fake. Santilli has made a great deal of money from the Roswell autopsy footage, and he still maintains that it is genuine. The rest of us will probably never know. The public's natural instinct is to question governmental denials, but the other options here are also so unreliable that it is very hard to determine the truth.

Tunguska Explosion

At 7:17AM ON 30th June 1908 there was a massive explosion in the atmosphere five miles above Siberia. It left the forest underneath burnt and charred, and pushed trees over in a 20-mile radius. It threw people to the floor and broke windowpanes 50 miles away. One hundred miles away, witnesses reported seeing the explosion create an enormous black cloud of ash which was accompanied by a terrific roar. This deafening noise was even heard 300 miles away, and all across the world scientific equipment recorded strange occurrences in northern Russia. To this day, bizarre growth patterns in plant and animal life can be found in the area. But what exactly happened in Tunguska that day?

The nearest witnesses to the explosion were reindeer herders 25 miles from the blast's epicentre. They were sleeping in their tents when the massive force blew them into the air. One man was reported to have died, and the others lost consciousness. When they came round, they saw the forest around them devastated and smouldering. Other witnesses at a trading post in Vanavara 50 miles south of the explosion, reported seeing the sky split in two, with the northern part covered in flames. A blast that washed over them was so hot it felt as if their clothes were on fire. It threw them 20 feet in the air, and when they regained their senses, a terrible crashing bang was followed by a noise which sounded like a downpour of small stones hitting the ground.

More distant witnesses had seen the phenomenon's final impressive act approaching. Residents in remote towns had seen a great 'ball of fire,' with an iridescent tail, streaking across the morning sky. Many thought it was the beginning of the great final apocalypse. The local newspaper, the Sibir, reported what was seen from the village of Nizhne-Karelinsk, 200 miles from the explosion:

'The peasants saw a body shining brightly – with a bluish white light. It moved vertically downwards for about ten minutes. The body was in the form of a 'pipe.' The sky was cloudless, except that low down on the horizon in the direction in which this glowing body was observed, a small dark cloud was noticed. It was hot and dry and when the shining body approached the ground it seemed to be pulverised, in its place a huge cloud of black smoke was formed and a loud crash, not like thunder, but as if from the fall of large stones, or from gunfire, was heard. All the buildings shook and at the same time, a forked tongue of flame broke through the cloud. The old women wept, everyone thought that the end of the world was approaching.'

The Russian authorities were not able to send anyone to investigate the phenomenon until March 1927, when Leonid Kulik was chosen by the Soviet Academy of Sciences to find out what had happened. Kulik arrived in the area and noticed the lines of trees all knocked down radiating from a distant point. He took photographs and studied the land, but was never able to find any fragments or meteorite rock samples. It seemed that whatever had caused the huge heavenly event had vaporised itself. The absence of physical remains left the Russians perplexed. They felt that only a massive rock from outer space could have caused those effects.

Following the dropping of atomic bombs on Japan during the Second World War, photographs comparing the devastation of Hiroshima and Nagasaki and the area near the epicentre of the Tunguska explosion displayed many similarities. A revision of eye-witness accounts also increased the possibility of the Russian phenomenon being a nuclear explosion. However, no nuclear weapons existed in 1908, so some people speculated the blast was caused by an alien space craft crashing to Earth.

Such an idea is now largely scoffed at, and has been replaced with theories of anti-matter or a black hole imploding above Siberia. Our improved scientific knowledge has been able to deduce that the explosion was the equivalent of a 40-megaton nuclear weapon. But Man's ideas about what caused this amazing event, whether it involves UFOs or other intergalactic oddities, requires an understanding of a subject that we still have not quite grasped.

UFO CRASHES

IN 1963, A SCIENTIST known as Fritz Werner was working on specialist nuclear tests in Arizona. In May of that year, Werner was asked to go on a specialist assignment – he was flown to Phoenix, and then taken by bus with a group of other men to a destination north-west of the city. The men were told not to talk to each other, and when unloaded from the vehicle they were shown a crash site. Werner claims that he saw a 30-feet-wide metal disc protruding from the desert sand. He was asked to calculate the speed of the impact, and says that during his time on site he also saw the body of a four-feet-tall creature wearing a silver suit in the medical tent. He was taken back to Arizona and made to sign the Official Secrets Act.

In 1957, a crashed UFO actually resulted in physical evidence being put into the public domain. On 18th September a journalist named Ibrahin Sued, who worked at a major Brazilian paper called O Globo, received a very odd letter. It was unsigned, but was said to be by a man who had been fishing near the town of Ubatuba in Sao Paulo, and saw a bizarre flying disc almost crash into the sea. The anonymous man said the craft was travelling at incredible speeds, and although it missed the water, it exploded in mid-air. The man managed to collect fragments from the strange vessel, which he included in the letter. These pieces were sent for official testing, and the Brazilian agricultural ministry declared it was a form of unusually pure magnesium. The results of experiments carried out by the Brazilian Army and Navy were kept secret.

Unlike more remote areas, the great advantage UFO researchers have when investigating odd incidents in America is that there are often plenty of witnesses. On 9th December 1965 hundreds of people saw a bizarre object streaking across the skies over Ohio and Pennsylvania. Some of the witnesses were airline pilots whose planes were shaken by the turbulence created by the unusual heavenly body. For six minutes, people watched what they thought was a meteorite travel from north-west to south-east before it seemed to explode. In fact, the object crashed in a wooded area in the town of Kecksberg, and started a small fire. Local police and fire authorities were unable to reach the site because they were turned away by a specialist military team who had immediately descended on the area. Witnesses said they had later seen the armed unit load a rounded metallic object onto a flatbed lorry which was then covered in tarpaulin to disguise its load.

Undoubtedly the most unsettling UFO crash and subsequent government reaction is reported to have occurred in northern Mexico, in the state of Chihuahua. UFO investigators have obtained documents which they claim reveal that an unidentified object was tracked by two US Air Defense radars on 25th August 1974. The object seemed to be entering the atmosphere from orbit, and was heading towards the United States, but veered off at the last minute and disappeared from sight over Mexico. At the same time, Mexican authorities said a light aeroplane had been lost over the area. The next day, Mexican search and rescue teams hunting for the downed plane started reporting that they had found the crash site, and two aircraft seemed to have been involved. When they transmitted a message that claimed the second appeared to be metallic and circular in shape, all broadcasts were ordered to stop.

UFO, or just poor photography?

UFO enthusiasts believe the US government heard these messages and immediately organised a response team. The US government strongly urged Mexico to accept their help, and when the local authorities ignored the offer, they decided to go in anyway. Mexican salvage squads had already loaded the two craft onto a truck and were heading south. By the time the US forces, travelling in helicopters, had caught up with them, a terrible tragedy had occurred. All the people with the convoy had somehow been mysteriously killed, so the American team, wearing protective clothing, took charge of the suspect air vehicle. They ferried it slung underneath a cargo helicopter, and took it to a secret installation in the US.

There is no absolute proof of UFO activity, but investigators continue to claim that more and more official evidence is being revealed that support these stories. The truth may not be 'out there,' but it could certainly lie hidden in the vaults of a government agency.

UFOS AND MILITARY INTERCEPTIONS

THE UFO PHENOMENON has an almost inextricable connection to the world's military forces. Many sceptics believe that a substantial amount of unexplained sightings are actually test flights of secret man-made fighters and bombers. Conspiracy theorists on the other hand are convinced the United States government in particular is in collusion with alien life forms – and that its military's high-technology weapons have been created with the aid of extraterrestrial intelligence.

One of the first eminent military witnesses of UFO sightings was Commander Robert B. McLaughlin of the US Navy. McLaughlin graduated as an engineer and researched guided missile systems in the 1940s. It was during his time spent as a rocket expert at White Sands, the military proving ground, that he witnessed an unknown flying structure for himself. In May 1949 he was watching the test of an upper atmosphere rocket, when he saw a white object travelling at a speed of about a mile a second, at an altitude of about 25 miles. Initially he thought it was the rocket experiencing a technical glitch, but the object speeded up to a velocity far in excess of normal craft. He noticed that the object left no vapour trails, and was similar in appearance, placement and motion to other phenomenon reported by staff at White Sands.

A year earlier, in January 1948, Captain Thomas Mantell was flying a F-51 Mustang

Watching the skies, but is the truth really out there?

in a group of four aircraft in the skies over Kentucky when he was asked by airforce command to investigate a strange object seen at a high altitude. In broad daylight Mantell flew after the target, but his plane inexplicably plunged to the ground. Subsequent investigators believe he had chased after a 'Skyhook' experimental balloon, but ran out of oxygen at high altitude. This does not entirely tally with Mantell's own last message, which revealed he had been approaching a massive metallic object. Whatever Mantell encountered, the US military placed increasing numbers of Air Force fighters at the ready to intersect any other strange flying craft, and the events surrounding many US lost planes in subsequent years were kept highly secret.

The British Royal Air Force has not had such a long history of events involving UFOs,

and the first really mysterious incident actually involved an American pilot. Captain William Schaffer was a US Air Force exchange officer flying an F6 Lightning over the North Sea. Radar stations picked up an unknown object, and Schaffer was dispatched to observe. He managed to close on it, but then contact was lost. Radar operators noticed the two blips of Schaffer's plane and the other object merged to form one, and then separated again. Radio controllers managed to reach Schaffer, who seemed confused. He was ordered to ditch the Lightning and wait for a rescue helicopter to retrieve him. Although other military aircraft witnessed Schaffer's controlled sea landing, and saw his plane's cockpit canopy open, he did not manage to escape. In a cloak of secrecy, the RAF raised the Lightning later that year, but few details have ever been released.

The most widespread and fascinating case of military involvement in a UFO case happened in Belgium. On 29th November 1989 hundreds of civilians reported seeing a huge dark grey triangular shape flying across then night sky. This sparked off massive interest in the country, and similar odd craft were seen across Europe. Then, in 1990, two Belgian Air Force F-16s actually managed to intercept the UFO, but it displayed amazing turns of speed and direction and broke the fighter's radar lock-on. The Belgian government and its military opened up all the data it recorded for public inspection, and it even pledged to have fighter planes on permanent stand-by for UFO watchers. The sightings gradually fell away, but scientists have continued to study the information gleaned during the period.

Episodes such as this support the theory that the world's military is, indeed, having aerial rendezvous with the other-worldly craft. Despite sceptical explanations, the sheer range of incidents, and expense and danger involved during them, suggest that governments view the subject seriously. It is claimed that between January and August 1996 the US Department of Defense secretly scrambled fighters up to 23 times for unknown flying objects. The Belgian authorities in the last case may seem candid and honest, but how much individual authorities know about possible alien invaders is another matter. Whilst various military organisations try to reveal little, the well documented reports of world-wide incidents point to the possibility that Man is, indeed, encountering UFOs firsthand.

EARTHLY ENERGIES AND MYSTICAL PLACES

EARTHLY ENERGY

SOME PEOPLE BELIEVE the earth has a natural source of energy that manifests itself as a magnetic field or electrical current. This unseen power is thought to have the ability to affect human bodily conditions and create biochemical reactions when people are near a prime spot of Earth Energy. Particularly potent areas are known as vortices, and many enthusiasts are of the opinion that these points help provide Man with rejuvenating or beneficial energy. As a sign of proof, they point to the idea that ancient races were more in tune with natural powers, and built important structures on sites emanating large amounts of energy. They claim Stonehenge, The Great Pyramid at Giza and Nazca are all points of strong natural forces.

As the idea of quantifiable, geophysical Earth power or natural energy has developed, the subject of ley-lines has very much caught the public's imagination. Although leys have significance based on historical and archaeo-logical fact, the theory of Earth Energy was brought about by New Age philosophies. Many enthusiasts have examined the subject with a scientific approach, despite it originating alongside many of the 'hippy' theories of the1960s and 70s. Certainly, many people do connect Earth Energy with ley-lines and mystical qualities, but there is also some scientific substance to the idea.

Actual hard evidence is scarce, despite enthusiasts' opinions. Dowsers suggest they can pick up strong sources of energy at many sacred sites, but that is a fact only as believable as dowsing itself. Earth Energy researchers often suggest that power centres are all areas heavily charged with negative ions, and there is an unusual state of electrical, magnetic or electromagnetic flux. They term the whole phenomenon 'geophysical anomalies,' and whilst it seems superficially impressive, the technological community is less convinced. Although many scientists are happy to entertain the possibility of untapped natural energy sources, they do not agree that many of these qualities attributed to Earth Energy have yet been proven.

CROP CIRCLES

THE PHENOMENON OF crop circles is one that we regard as being a relatively recent mystery, but strange patterns have actually been appearing in fields for over three hundred years. Sometimes occurring in sand, ice or even snow, five thousand of these beautiful geometric shapes have manifested themselves in over forty countries across the globe. However, Man is still no closer to realising their significance. Some are undoubtedly hoaxes but what do the others mean? Are they messages from space, Mother Earth, or perhaps another dimension?

Over the years, those who live in the countryside, particularly those who live along ley lines and channels of natural

Crop circle; although many are perpetrated by hoaxers, the difference between hoax and genuine circles is clear.

energy, have come to regard the circles as part of rural life and a few witnesses have actually seen them made. They say an invisible line snakes its way at high speed through a field, pushing the stalks of crops aside. When it reaches a certain point it begins to spin round, pushing the crop down radially, as would the hands on a clock. When it has turned the full 360 degrees the force just vanishes, leaving the crop perfectly matted on the field floor. No stalks spring up, and no stalks are crushed, they are all carefully and permanently bowed.

The question as to who or what actually determines that the patterns should be made is still up for debate. Tales of UFOs and odd lights above fields the night before new formations appear are common. Similarly, there are a substantial proportion of hoax circles, but these are often easily discernible as they have trampled, crushed crops rather than gently bent stalks. Many people are convinced freak weather conditions such as mini, localised whirlwinds cause the patterns. There is also a continuing study into the scientific qualities of crop circles, where investigators hope a rational, serious approach will reveal the truth.

Perhaps the most popular explanation for the appearance of crop circles is connected with earth forces. The great majority of good, reputable patterns in England appear in Wiltshire, around historic areas of high natural energy. They also often occur close to ancient forts, burial mounds, standing stones and fertility symbols therefore suggesting an affiliation with Britain's traditional heritage. Indeed, many people are convinced the ancient forces of Mother Earth have a hand in their creation.

An aspect of crop circles' character that is not questionable is the effect they have on electronic equipment. Tape recorders are known to speed up once inside a circle and then slow down again outside. State-of-the-art video equipment malfunctions without good cause, and even ordinary photographic cameras have produced severely distorted images. A rather ironic reaction circles have is on farm machinery. Not only are good crops flattened during a circle's production, but many farmers have witnessed their harvesting equipment refusing to work anywhere near the circles.

The circles have striking effects on humans. Some experts suggest that stepping inside certain patterns can cause extreme emotion change. Some people feel an improved physical well-being and vitality in certain circles, whilst in others feelings of nausea, migraine, fatigue and light-headedness can be brought about. Just by sitting inside stone circles people with a long standing medical conditions are said to have been significantly improved or even cured; the effect of a crop circle's power on animals is equally impressive. Horses and cats in particular become agitated near patterns, and often refuse to enter them. Flocks of birds have been seen flying straight towards a crop formation, only to drastically steer around them at the last minute, whilst some dogs feel compelled to bound right into the centre of some circles, only to drop down asleep when they reach it.

It seems a shame that some people do create hoax crop circles. Of all unexplained phenomena, they are one of the most deserving of scientific study. Unlike the fleeting images of monsters, aliens and ghosts, crop circles are their own record of some unknown power. Whatever causes these formations undoubtedly leaves a trace of its inexplicable force. Country folk are well aware that, for centuries, something with which they have grown to live has been going on in their fields, but it is still something they do not quite understand.

CRYSTALS

THE NEW AGE movement has placed great emphasis on one particular type of power instrument – crystals. These attractive chemical solidifications are now regarded as being the wonder substance of New Age belief, and have permeated into the world of popular culture. The celebrity world is awash with high-profile, spiritually-aware people who attest to the positive power of crystals. They believe these substances direct and control energy flows in the body and promote physical and emotional well-being. But do crystals really provide magical support for people or is this effect merely an unsubstantiated craze?

A crystal is a solid 'rock' created by chemicals solidifying in a solution. Its chemical construction is particularly special because it is formed by regularly repeating patterns of atoms and molecules, and the crystal particle is pulled together by flat external forces. Like snowflakes, they are a naturally occurring phenomenon where each one created is unique, and crystals occur in any number of shapes. They are highly aesthetic and prized for use in clothing and jewellery.

Throughout history, crystals have also been regarded as having magic properties and were often believed to hold bizarre paranormal powers. Ancient races considered crystals to contain the power of Mother Earth as they originated in its crust, and the energy of the sun because they were seen to reflect light in bizarre ways. Crystals were also supposed to show the future and give people superhuman powers, with the use of crystal balls by psychics being a deliberate choice.

Crystals like these are claimed by many to have mysterious healing powers.

Modern New Age enthusiasts believe the power of the crystals lies in their ability to regulate, calm and heal the body. They are believed to channel good energy, ward off bad energy and are also said to 'vibrate' at frequencies which compliment natural body functions. Lifestyle gurus declare that crystals promote self-expression, meditation and creativity, and that a full compliment of different crystals is needed to engage with all a person's needs.

Different crystals are said to affect the body in different ways. Amethysts are believed to help headaches, eye and hair problems, balance blood sugar levels, increase psychic abilities and reduce anger, impatience and nightmares. Emeralds apparently increase the efficiency of a body's respiration, heart and blood systems, lift depression and insomnia and evoke peace, harmony, patience and love. Finally, diamonds increase clarity, confidence and trust, clarify attitudes and thoughts and develop prosperity, generosity and love.

What better reason could there be for buying them for a loved one?

In recent years it has been fashionable to employ crystals in jewellery, not only for aesthetic qualities, but so as to have beneficial power sources near the body. A chiropractor called Charles Brown developed the Bioelectric Shield – a piece of jewellery that has crystals arranges in such a way that they protect people from all the many harmful electromagnetic forces in the modern world: mobile phones, computer screens and power lines. These 'shields' are said to be medically proven, and are even worn by Cherie Blair, the wife of the British Prime Minister. The different constructions of these shields are said to provide protection for different things.

Unfortunately, these assertions are not based on any sort of scientific basis. Indeed they are based on nothing more than blind faith. Sceptics believe any reaction they do have on human beings is the result of selective or wishful thinking, more self-deception and placebo effect. But crystals do have many vital roles in our modern world. They are important components in electronic, optical and communication industries, and feature in many types of high-tech equipment. These functions are due to one special function that crystals really do have. In 1880 Pierre and Jacques Curie realised that certain crystals produce an electrical change when they are compressed. This discovery was termed the 'piezoelectric effect,' and now crystals are used for highly scientific purposes.

However, the piezoelectric effect has no effect on the human body, and crystals provide no protection from illness, calamity or misfortune. That does not detract from their beauty, but as far as science is concerned the magical power of crystals is completely unfounded.

EARTH LIGHTS

THROUGHOUT HISTORY, PEOPLE have noted strange lighting phenomena emanating from remote areas of natural land. 'Will-o'-the-wisps' are well known occurrences featuring small flames that spark from marsh and woodland. Ball lightning is a curious form of meteorological phenomenon where air pressure causes an electrical charge in the form of a ball. But the most fascinating natural lights are even more bizarre. People across the world have reported seeing strange orbs of light that seem to ignore the standard laws of physics – explanations for their appearance are anything but definite. Present theories range from alien spacecraft to pan-dimensional energy. All we do know is that they seem to appear from the ground, and so they have been termed Earth Lights.

These odd glowing visions have been witnessed radiating all manner of colours, from bright white, to blue, red or even black. They can be as small as a tennis ball, or as large as a car, and although they are normally spherical, witnesses have seen Earth Lights of many designs. Accounts of glowing tadpole shapes are particularly common. People who have managed to view them close-up report odd internal reactions, and bizarre crackling noises. The lights move in erratic directions, and can split into formations of multiple floating orbs. They seem to have a strong connection to geological and geographical features, and linger around lakes, mountains and rocky ridges.

One of the most impressive series of sightings happened in Hessdalen, Norway, in the early 1980s. People living in the area began to see strange lights emerging from the valley in November 1981. The glowing designs ranged from bullet shapes to triangles, and were commonly white and yellow in colour. The level of reports reached such a pitch that two airforce officers were sent by the Norwegian government to examine the occurrences. By the start of 1984, Swedish and Norwegian

UFO enthusiasts had begun Project Hessdalen, a month long scientific study of the valley. This yielded some readings of Earth Light properties and also managed to capture examples of the Earth Light phenomenon on film.

Although the 1960s saw the creation of theories that connected these unexplained light displays with earthquakes and fault lines, in-depth study of the subject had always been overshadowed by alien and UFO interest. However, unlike UFOs, the verifiable scientific relationship between these lights and the earth has allowed the phenomenon to be quietly, but seriously, studied. The leading name in this field is Paul Devereux, the man who actually coined the term 'Earth Lights.' Devereux has

Earth lights dance above a Norwegian fjord. These are probably similar to the Northern Lights in origin.

travelled the world studying versions of the phenomenon, separating fake or mistaken incidents from genuine Earth Lights. His conclusion is that they are an honest and real phenomenon.

Devereux, along with much of the interested scientific community, believes the lights may be connected with the strains and conflicting energy found in the Earth's crust. Just as heavy pressure in the atmosphere causes storms and lightning, so too pressure under the surface causes equally impressive reactions. As the tectonic plates rise and fall, it is suggested that energy is released through particular areas of weakness such as fault lines, or areas of high mineral or rock density. It has been discovered that many historical accounts of strange lights appeared on recently discovered fault lines, or just before earthquakes developed.

Different theories suggest the lights could be alien landing craft; some alien abduction victims have reported seeing similar glowing features. Other people believe they have amazing paranormal qualities, and link our world with another dimension. Some witnesses claim to have heard ghostly voices and seen apparitions after an Earth Light display. In both these cases the effect of magnetic variation on brain patterns has been cited as having an influence. Many experts believe the extreme magnetic upheaval caused by conflicting tectonic forces needed in Earth Light creation may cause the brain to suffer hallucinations.

The effect on witnesses, although not dangerous, can be striking. One of the most common areas for Earth Light incidents in Britain is the Longendale Valley in the Peak District. Sean Wood is a local resident who has seen the lights over thirty times in sixteen years. As a catalogue of his sightings he now produces paintings of the local landscapes. In all his pictures, in the corner of a field or the side of a valley, there lurks the image of a small glowing orb. For him, the phenomenon of Earth Lights is an unexplainable, but acceptable, natural occurrence.

Ley Lines

THE TERM, 'LEY-LINE,' was invented by Alfred Watkins, a British business-man. In 1921 he was looking for interesting features in a regional map when he noticed that many ancient and sacred sites could be placed on a straight line running through the countryside. As he researched the subject more, Watkins discovered that these mysterious lines could be identified, not just by marker points, but that some were physically visible from the ground. The lines were anything from two to several miles long and their reference points were objects like ancient churches, standing stones, stone circles and prehistoric burial sites. In 1922 Watkins published his first book, Early British Trackways, which explained his initial thoughts on the subject. He published his seminal work, The Old Straight Track, which fully demonstrated his new-found phenomenon, in 1952.

Watkins used the term 'ley-lines' or 'leys' as it came from an old Saxon word for cleared glade. He believed they were trading routes for Neolithic Man who used ancient surveying techniques to create long, straight lines. His theory followed the thinking that many areas on these routes became sacred sites, and over time the pathways fell into disuse, leaving only the special points discernible. He also believed that many of the ancient, pagan holy sites were later commandeered and Christianised, leaving a fascinating mixture of both prehistorical and relatively recent points of interest along the lines.

Despite the fact that these paths followed a perfectly straight line, which often meant cutting through forests, climbing up valleys or running across hilltops, Watkins maintained his belief that they were trading routes. By 1929 he had stopped referring to the old leys, simply calling them 'old straight tracks.' Watkins died in 1935 but his idea had instigated the formation of the Straight Track Club, a collection of interested enthusiasts based across Britain who enjoyed investigating their own regional versions of ley lines.

Many people felt that the difficult routes taken by leys running through steep or testing countryside meant they were unlikely to be pathways for traders – other theories about their nature was put forward. In 1936 a British writer called Dion Fortune first suggested the idea that ancient sites could be linked by lines of mysterious cosmic forces. A member of the Straight Line Club, Arthur Lawton, continued with this notion in 1938. Lawton was a dowser, and had been fascinated by German and French dowsing theories that were connected with standing stones, so he formulated the idea that leys were lines of natural energy that could be proven by dowsing.

During the Second World War the Straight Line Club and its activities dwindled, but in the 1950s new ideas about leys burst into the public's consciousness. Various UFO books from France and America linked the flying saucer phenomenon with lines of cosmic force. In 1961, Tony Wedd, a British ley hunter and ex-pilot, published his theory that leys were magnetic flight paths for alien visitors, and any sites of interest found along them acted as landmarks. From Wedd's work, the modern movement in ley research truly began when in 1969 another enthusiast, John Michell, wrote The View Over Atlantis, a book that combined ley lines, earth energy, UFOs and ancient mathematics. The 1960s and 70s saw all manner of New Age theories, and leys began to be automatically associated with lines of energy, flying saucers and strange psychic experiences.

The phenomenon spread across the world, and New Age enthusiasts were eager to seize the idea of cosmic forces and aliens wholeheartedly. The city of Seattle in the USA even readily gave a $5,000 grant for a group of dowsers to create a ley line map of the area. To some extent they missed the original point of ley lines, which was they were straight routes connecting sites of sacred interests. In fact, the United States has its own version of Watkins-style leys. Native American 'Spirit-Lines' found across the country are believed to have been ancient sacred pathways. Similar features are found in Mexico, and it has been suggested the Nazca lines may be a variation on the same theme.

So the real significance of leys is still unknown. Although the theories and background ideas have bred and multiplied, few people have discovered more ley line facts than Alfred Watkins. His vision is still the most fact based and, despite its shortcomings, still the most plausible. It would be a shame to see the phenomenon of ley lines become synonymous with extreme New Age ideas because it has a fascinating historical and geographical background that has not yet been fully studied

THE BERMUDA TRIANGLE

THE BERMUDA, or Devil's, Triangle is an area of ocean found off the southeastern tip of the United States. It is a region of water indelibly connected with mysterious vessel disappearances; the popular perception is that countless boats and planes have been inexplicably lost there. The triangle extends from Bermuda to Miami and then to the Puerto Rico, and is said to contain a supernatural secret. Some high profile disappearances have occurred there, and the notion of its existence has been turned into a modern myth in the media. Even the term 'Bermuda Triangle' was coined in a fictional publication. But does the sea here really house some unknown power that pulls sea and airmen to their doom, or is this mystery based mainly on imagination?

The most famous loss in the triangle is known as the mystery of Flight 19, and happened on 5th December 1945. A squadron of five US Navy Avenger torpedo bombers set off from their base in Fort Lauderdale, Florida to conduct a practice mission over the island of Bimini. The flight contained 14 men, all of them students apart from the commander, Lt Charles Taylor. About an hour and a half after the mission began, radio operators received a signal from Taylor saying his compasses were not working, but he believed he was over the Florida Keys. He was advised to fly north which would bring him back to the mainland. In fact, he was over the Bahamas, and his attempts to head north and north-east merely took him further away from solid ground. A terrible storm that day hampered communications and it seems Taylor rejected a suggestion to pass control of the squadron to one of the other pilots.

Radio contact was entirely lost and search craft were dispatched to try and find the flight to guide them back in. Of the three planes used to rescue Flight 19, one lost communications itself because of an iced over aerial, one was just unsuccessful whilst another seemed to explode shortly after take-off. Flight 19 itself has never been found, but it is assumed that they ditched into the raging sea when their fuel ran out, with the heavy planes rapidly sinking to the ocean floor. The US Navy recorded that the disaster was caused by Taylor's confusion, but an appeal by his family had this overturned, and a verdict of 'causes or reasons unknown' was given. However, Flight 19 is not the only high profile official loss in the area, and the USS Cyclops and Marine Sulphur Queen have also disappeared without trace.

The legend of Flight 19 was cemented by its inclusion in Steven Spielberg's Close Encounters of the Third Kind movie. Indeed, some theories state that visiting UFO craft enter an underwater base in the Bermuda area, and they have been the cause of the disappearances. Other fantastical ideas such as technologies from Atlantis or evil marine creatures have also been considered. Some people even suggest the triangle is the site of a gateway into another dimension. Strange oceanographic features such as huge clouds of methane gas escaping from the seabed have also been blamed for the disappearances.

In reality, the triangle does have one natural quality which may contribute to the losses. Unlike everywhere else in the world – apart from the Dragon's Triangle near Japan – compasses point to true north rather than magnetic north. This may be a contributing factor to the triangle's legend, but the US Coastguard officially believes the losses are caused by a mixture of environmental and man-made mistakes. This region is used by a large amount of ocean and air traffic, much of which is navigated by inexperienced pleasure-seekers. A strong Gulf Stream and unpredictable weather conditions not only cause vessels to run into trouble, but also remove many traces of them once they have been wrecked.

It is interesting also to note that the coastguard does not view the area as having a particularly high incidence of accidents. One researcher examined many historic losses in the triangle. He came to the conclusion that rumours and elaboration had clouded the real, understandable, causes behind the events. Similarly, the international insurers, Lloyds of London, have records that demonstrate that this region near Bermuda is no more treacherous than any other waterway. However, the myth of the Bermuda Triangle is so strong it will live on as long as fictional writers use it as a site of mysterious happenings.

THE DRAGON'S TRIANGLE

THE BERMUDA TRIANGLE'S infamous association with disappearing boats and aircraft is known across the globe. Less well known is an area off the west coast of Japan which has an equally deadly history. It is an area where Japanese sailors fear to voyage; they call it 'Ma-no Uni' – the 'Sea of the Devil.' Legend has it that huge restless dragons surface from their deep shelters to seize any unfortunate passing mariners. Japanese sailors have often recorded freakish occurrences in the area and talk of hearing terrible noises and seeing awful red lights. They believe one particularly potent creature lives in an immense palace beneath the waves. They call this monster 'Li-Lung,' the 'Dragon King of the Western Sea,' and say his lair is decorated with the ships he has captured.

This mysterious zone stretches from western Japan to Yap island in the south and Taiwan to the west. Like the Bermuda Triangle, it has an above-average rate of navigation and communication failures. In truth, this area of ocean bears a remarkable resemblance to its Western cousin. Both areas are known for extreme changes in weather conditions, unexpected fogs, tidal waves, seaquakes and hurricanes, and both have examples of agonic lines. Their most unwelcome similarities are the truly horrifying levels of unexplained sinkings and disappearances.

By the late 1940s, the amount of ships being lost without trace in the region lead to the Japanese government declaring the area a danger zone. In the early 1950s they decided to dispatch a research vessel to study the area. Despite enjoying good visibility and calm seas, the Kiao Maru No.5 disappeared without trace on 24th September 1952. The lives of all twenty-two crew and nine scientists were lost. The vessel has never been found. It has only been in relatively recent years that these incidents of strange disappearances have been reported in the West. To the Japanese, they are regular occurrences which stretch back for centuries and continue to this day. Whether it is dragons or not, the real evidence behind this ocean's terrible secret remains on the seabed.

Easter Island

EASTER ISLAND, or Rapa Nui, is in the south Pacific Ocean and lies about 2,300 miles from the west coast of Peru. Formed by a volcanic eruption on the ocean floor, it is separated from the other Polynesian islands by huge expanses of sea. The island itself only occupies 45 square miles, and has three volcanic craters. Now lakes, they are some of the few areas of fertile nature, for the rest of the island is rather desolate and barren. However, it has not always been like this, and there remains evidence that the land was once rich in flora and fauna.

The first time the outside world knew about Easter Island was when a Dutch admiral called Jakob Roggeveen stumbled across it on Easter Sunday, 1722. When he landed, he found a backward race which lived in caves and rudimentary huts, and practised cannibalism. What truly amazed him were the huge stone carved figures, or 'moai,' that stood on guard around the island. Modern investigations have revealed there are something like a thousand of these great statues, standing between 12 and 25 feet high, and weighing up to 20 tonnes. The largest one is 65 feet tall and weighs 90 tonnes. However, when Roggeveen stepped ashore, many of these figures had been torn down by the fierce natives.

The origin of the Easter Island race is an issue of contention. One early visitor to the island after Roggeveen was Captain James Cook. Cook had a Hawaiian sailor aboard his ship who could understand the Easter Island native tongue. This suggested that they spoke Polynesian, and indeed the general consensus is that they were descended from a distant Polynesian tribe. There is also a celebrated theory that they actually came from South America which is supported by the fact that bulrushes and sweet potatoes found on the island were said to be imports from that continent. There were also considerable similarities between pre-Inca

Measuring statues on Easter Island. The origins of the people who created the statues remains shrouded in mystery.

American cultures and the examples of Easter Island culture, although it is believed there may have been an early trading industry between Easter Island, South America and the Polynesian Islands.

The Easter Island race probably settled on the island sometime around the middle of the first millennium AD, and began building their statues quite soon afterwards. The early Easter Islanders developed a precise technique for creating the stone men out of the walls of the volcanic craters. Using a system of logs and ropes, they would sit the moai on a funerary platform, called an 'ahu,' under which the remains of dead elders were buried. It is believed the stone figure acted as a talisman, guarding and protecting the clan of the dead islander, although some experts suggest the islanders ended up erecting the

statues purely for the joy of making them. Archaeologists have also discovered wooden tablets called 'talking boards,' which describe ancient religious rites of the old culture.

The Easter Island story is the archetypal island version of paradise lost. When the first Polynesian immigrants landed on the island it was a land of bountiful natural produce. There were great forests, sugar beet crops, exotic fruit and native meat sources. In these conditions the people flourished. They built fine houses and enjoyed life, but in around AD 1500 a new cult called 'Makemake' or 'the cult of the birdman' sprang up. This may have signalled the arrival of a new tribe from across the sea, and soon afterwards overpopulation and wasteful island management caused the

Are the stone heads on Easter Island memorials to ancestors, or guardians of the island?

crops to fail and the natural resources to be depleted. The different clans and tribes began warring, even overturning each other's statues, and legend on the island recounts a terrible battle between tribes of 'long ears' and a tribe of 'short ears.'

Within a couple of centuries, Easter Island was the barren waste populated by savages discovered by Roggeveen. The life of islanders only grew worse. The inter-tribal conflicts continued until 1862, when ships arrived and enslaved a thousand of the island's fit men to work in the Peruvian mining industry. These islanders quickly grew ill in the strange continent, and the few that returned home brought back diseases. Smallpox and leprosy reduced the native population to 111 by 1877. European missionary workers helped the people of Easter Island survive, but many of the secrets of the island's strange stone faces were lost forever.

THE PYRAMIDS OF GIZA

THE ANCIENT EGYPTIANS believed that after mortal death the soul or spirit would continue life in another dimension. They buried their Pharaoh kings, who they regarded as living Gods, with all the treasures and objects needed to survive in comfort in the afterlife. They also embalmed their bodies to ensure that their mortal remains would be mummified and preserved for whatever fate awaited them. Crucially, they built impressive burial structures to demonstrate the dead person's importance and to aid their ascendancy to the next dimension in the heavens. The most famous and enigmatic of these buildings are Egypt's pyramids, and the most mystical of all these is the Great Pyramid of Cheops at Giza. However, many people question whether the structure really is just a simple, albeit awesome, tomb or whether the design holds one of the great secrets of civilisation.

The pyramids were erected between 2800 BC and 2200BC; the first was built by King Zoser in Saqqara near Memphis. Although the structure was created with six stepped tiers, and is not a strict pyramid as such, it was the first building designed exclusively to house the property and remains of the king. In the following centuries King Seneferu built his own trio of pyramids. One at Maidum was called the 'False Pyramid' because it was abandoned mid-project due to a structural weakness. One at Dahshur was known as the 'Bent Pyramid' because of another design problem which meant the gradient of its sides had to be reduced as it was constructed. The final one, called the 'Northern Pyramid of Seneferu,' was built

The pyramids of Egypt possess a haunting quality that stays with whoever sees them.

close to the 'Bent Pyramid,' and is recognised as the first true pyramid.

The most impressive structure, however, was completed around 2500 BC for King Cheops at a site in Giza, ten miles south of the city we now know as Cairo. Using an estimated 4000 builders, and tens of thousands more manual labourers, the 'Great Pyramid' stands 481 feet high. It is believed it may have taken up to 30 years to quarry and assemble the two and a half million blocks of limestone, which weigh a total of six million tonnes. The base of the pyramid covers an area just over 30 acres. It appears that great care was lavished on Cheops' structure, and although later pyramids were

built for King Chephren and King Mycerinus alongside, neither is of the same quality.

Certainly, there are many fascinating aspects of the Great Pyramid's design. Its sides run perfectly north to south and east to west to within a tenth of a degree. The base is an almost exact square, with an error margin of just seven inches, whilst the pavement around the structure is level to within an inch. Unlike other pyramids, this one houses a great number of chambers and corridors, with the lengthy 345 feet long Ascending Passageway running directly north. It had been widely assumed that the pyramid stood as a great monument to hold the body and treasures of King Cheops,

Does the layout of the pyramids really reflect the position of the stars 5,000 years ago?

Guardian of the Pyramids: the Sphinx remains as enigmatic today as it was to our ancestors.

although when the structure was first opened by Caliph Abdullah al Mamun in AD820 nothing was found inside. Al Mamun discovered the King's Chamber blocked by three huge granite plugs, which he and his men circumvented. But when they arrived in the great room, there simply stood an empty stone sarcophagus.

The mystery of what had happened to the pyramid after its completion, if its assumed use is correct, has continued to this day. In the absence of real evidence of burial ceremonies in the structure, many fantastic other theories have grown. Some people believe it was built by God either as a stone version of the Bible, or as a record containing references to all events past, present and future. They believe that the various passageways represent historical time-lines, and intersections between them mark great happenings. The birth of Christ and the two World Wars are supposed to be signified along these routes. Some experts who advocate this theory said it also showed a Second Coming in 1881 and the end of the world in 1953. Other mathematical studies of the Great Pyramid claims it demonstrates knowledge of the true value of pi, and was build using the 'sacred inch.'

A popular theory originating in the latter part of the last century is at the Great Pyramid was constructed by alien visitors. It has been proposed that these aliens did everything from creating Mankind to erecting the pyramid as a landing beacon for their next visit to Earth. Another well-known idea is called the Orion Theory and was created by Robert Bauval and Adrian Gilbert. They believe the pyramids at Giza are an earthly representation of the three stars in the Orion Nebula. The shafts found in the Great Pyramid are supposed to correlate with important astronomical features visible at the time of the building's construction. The Orion Theory states that the Ancient Egyptians were direct descendants of alien visitors, and retained some of their knowledge. The purpose of these important design features in their tombs was to help point the spirit of the dead back towards the stars from whence they came.

Many of these 'ancient astronaut' theories suggest the pyramids were built around 10,000 years ago, rather than the 5,000 supported by historians. Other theories state that the instigating race may not have been aliens, but a now-lost civilisation. One writer, Edgar Cayce, was convinced the pyramids were built around 10,000 BC by travellers from Atlantis. However, his assertion that the Atlanteans also recorded the Second Coming of Christ in 1998 in the design of the pyramid, is somewhat flawed. Some theories even suggest that our conception of the chronology of the pyramids is wrong. Some people believe the build quality of the pyramids actually deteriorated, instead of improved, as the initial knowledge brought by the instigating race was lost over time.

Although the Great Pyramid has been explored and studied more than any other ancient structure in Egypt, new discoveries are constantly being made. In 1954 a previously unknown sealed pit was found on the south side, containing a 140 ft long cedar boat, which may have been buried to help the king travel to the after-life. In recent years, space equipment and remote controlled probes have been used to examine the building in ways never before possible. However, NASA's refusal to publish underground readings taken by the space shuttle, and the Egyptian government's unhelpful attitudes towards deeper exploration, has only increased conspiracy theories and myths of hidden secrets. For the world's interested public, the mystery of the Great Pyramid at Giza is as unknown today as when Caliph Abdullah al Mamun first reopened it over a millennium ago.

STONEHENGE

STONEHENGE LIES ON Salisbury Plain in the county of Wiltshire, England. The whole area is known to be mystical, with an abundance of ley lines, and is widely accepted as the centre of the crop circle phenomenon. Stonehenge itself was constructed in three stages. The first began in about 3,000BC, when a circular ditch was dug around the site and a raised bank two yards high and 106 yards in diameter was formed. Just inside the bank, 56 shallow holes were dug and then refilled and the first rock, the 'Heel Stone,' was introduced. This was positioned to mark the axis of sunrise at the summer solstice. Two smaller entrance stones were put in place, then 40 wooden posts, marking positions of the sun, were erected.

In around 2,000BC, a two-mile avenue to the River Avon was created. From southwest Wales, the builders imported 82 'bluestones,' weighing over four tonnes each. To reach the

Sacred circle: Stonehenge predates the Druids by almost two millenia, however.

Were the standing stones witness to blood sacrifice by their Stone Age builders?

site they would have had to travel 240 miles over land and water. These bluestones were used to construct a double circle inside the site. It is believed the builders never finished this design because they already had the idea to erect the third, and most impressive, phase.

This started in around 1900BC, with the selection of 75 loose blocks of sandstone, known as sarsens, from Avebury, 20 miles away. Using rollers and ropes, these 25-tonne, 17-feet-long rocks were pulled to the

site where they were then shaped and lifted into upright positions. The architectural detail of this stage is phenomenal, and the lintel stones that cap the pillars are actually curved to fit in the large circle. The Welsh bluestones were repositioned, and the structure was complete.

In each stage, the stones were placed at specific points demonstrating the position of the sun and moon at important times. The site was in continual use until about 1,000BC, but we still do not know exactly what it was used for. Very little human or cultural debris has been found on the site, so there can be no definitive answers.

Some experts say that this absence of historic litter leads to the suggestion that the structure was a temple or sacred site. Many of the other 900 stone circles in Britain served many uses and were often meeting places, so they often have remnants of ancient day-to-day life. Similarly, the amount of trouble endured, and the sheer scale of the project, indicates that Stonehenge was something of immense importance. The bluestones brought from Wales were exceedingly valuable to the Ancient Britons, and were ideal for a temple.

The possibility that it was partly used as a burial site has also been considered – during limited excavations it was discovered that the 56 shallow holes dug during the first phase contained cremated bones. There are also barrows, or burial tombs, of later Bronze Age warriors dotted around the outlying area.

Because of Stonehenge's obvious correlation to important astronomical events, a whole host of other theories have arisen. It may have been used as an observatory, or even a gigantic lunar calendar. In 1965, Gerald S. Hawkins, an astronomer at Boston University, published a book entitled Stonehenge Uncoded. In it, he claimed a computer had proven that Stonehenge marked many astronomical alignments. He even went so far as to say that Stonehenge was a computer itself, designed by the Ancient Britons to read the stars and calculate upcoming eclipses, but many experts feel he has not discovered the true significance of the structure.

In the seventeenth century historians believed the structure had been built by ancient Celtic priests, and many modern druids feel it is their right to perform rituals and ceremonies at the site. They are now no longer allowed to, and for good reason. Not only was damage occurring to the area, but modern druids have no connection to their Celtic namesakes. Anyway, Stonehenge was built around 1000 years before the Celtic druids existed.

Unfortunately, in the last few hundred years many of the stones have been stolen, lost or collapsed, and poor restoration work has been performed on some of the stones that remain. But the magic of the site and the design never dissipates. One legend says the most famous of all Britain's magicians, Merlin, summoned the stones and set them in place. It is a story in keeping with the mystical tradition of the area. Maybe the simple fact is that modern minds have just not imagined the true use of the site yet.

STONE CIRCLES AT CASTLERIGG

IF STONEHENGE IS THE most famous stone circle in Britain, the Castlerigg Stone Circle, near Keswick in the Lake District, must be the most atmospheric. Situated in an open bowl between rolling hills, this Megalithic construction appears as a perfect picture postcard. This is the land of Wordsworth, Coleridge and Romantic poetry; but many millennia before, it was home to an equally creative race.

The Castlerigg Stone Circle, also known as Keswick Carle or Druid's Circle, is one of the oldest in Britain. It was built in around 3,000BC and comprises 38 stones of various heights placed in a slightly oval shape. The largest stone is over eight feet tall, but the majority of them are less than five feet high. Although five of the stones have collapsed, it is a site in remarkably good condition.

It has a feature unique among stone circles in Britain. Inside the ring of rocks, ten smaller stones are placed in a rectangle in an

Amidst the rugged splendour of the Lake District, the Castlerigg circle is particularly imposing.

arrangement called 'The Cave.' There is also a slight mound in the centre, which, it has been suggested, is a burial chamber. However, the site has never been properly excavated, and perfunctory archaeological studies have only ever uncovered charcoal deposits.

Like Stonehenge, the site has qualities which make it suitable for use as an astronomical observatory, although an un-polished stone blade found near the circle suggests it may have been used as a centre of trade for the area's Neolithic axe industry. There is also a local legend that says the stones were never built to any design, but were actually men turned to rock by fear of a local monster.

In all likelihood, it probably formed a focal point for the local community, and may have been used for a combination of commercial, religious and tribal purposes. For now, we can only admire the stunning sight of this early man-made structure placed in an area of unique natural beauty.

HIDDEN CITIES AND LOST CIVILISATIONS

ATLANTIS

OUR KNOWLEDGE OF THE world's most famous lost continent comes from the work of one man – Plato. The great Greek philosopher was the singular source of all information about the ill-fated island race and whilst experts write long-winded theses about the age and position of Atlantis, nobody is entirely sure that Plato did not just invent the Atlantean people as an allegory for what happens when a civilisation over-reaches itself. Despite this, the hunt for Atlantis is as fierce as ever.

Plato lived in Greece between 428 and 348BC, and revealed the story of Atlantis in his dialogues 'Timeaus' and 'Critias'. Many of Plato's fables were fictional creations used to illustrate a point, but the history of Atlantis was repeatedly stated as fact. The dialogues recount the story of Solon, a Greek scholar who travelled to Egypt in around 600BC to learn more about the ancient world. The Egyptians were known to have knowledge and records dating back centuries, and as Solon tried to impress his hosts with tales of Greece's achievements, the wise old Egyptian priests put him in his place. They revealed a story about a continent and a people completely unknown to him.

Around 10,000BC, a powerful race lived on an island in the west, beyond the 'Gates of Hercules,' now believed to be the Straits of Gibraltar. The island was the kingdom of Poseidon, the Sea God. It had a huge central mountain with a temple dedicated to the deity, and lush outlying districts, there was an elaborate system of canals to irrigate its successful farms, and a bustling central city. The island was rich in vegetables, and was home to different types of exotic animals.

The Atlanteans were originally a powerful but fair race. They were an advanced people with a prosperous trading industry, a strong and noble army and a highly educated, cultured society. Their influence reached far and wide, and they controlled large areas of Africa, Asia and the Mediterranean. Although the island left its inhabitants wanting for nothing, their taste for power and empire led to them over-extending themselves. An attempt to conquer Athens failed, and the Atlanteans retreated home to face a cataclysmic disaster. Legend says that the great god Zeus saw the corruption that had seized the island's people, and sent down upon them an immense barrage of earthquakes, fire and water. Atlantis disappeared under the waves.

Whilst Plato's story was well known, the renewed modern interest in Atlantis began in 1882 with the publication of 'Atlantis: The Antediluvian World' by a American former congressman, Ignatius Donnelly. Donnelly's book was a mixture of conjecture, misinterpreted fact and actual history. But there were some interesting ideas; he noted similarities in the science and culture of native races which apparently could never have met. Likewise, the great ancient flood, which is said to have destroyed Atlantis, is logged in ancient writings and traditions of peoples around the world.

Exactly who the Atlanteans were is unknown. Some say they were aliens, some

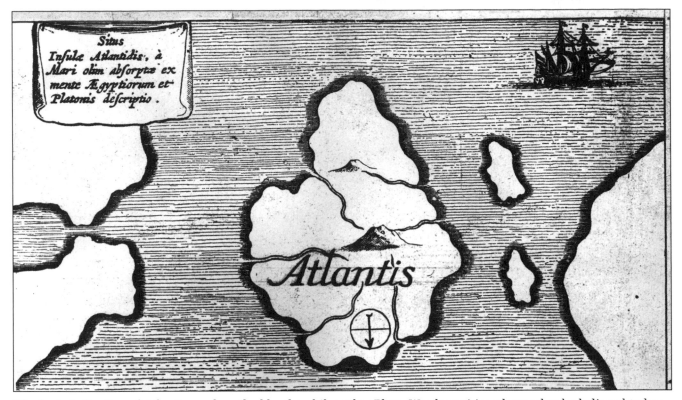

The lost civilisation of Atlantis, as described by the philosopher Plato. Was he writing about what he believed to be a real city, or was he simply describing an ideal state?

believe they were descendants of Lemuria, and some say they eventually travelled westward and became Native American tribes. Similarly, the actual placing of Atlantis is a subject open to argument. Many experts suggest the island was actually in the Mediterranean, and a constant stream of archaeological investigations in the area has tried to prove this.

There are theories that Sardinia in the Mediterranean, and the island of Thera in the Aegean Sea, could be Atlantis. Both had highly-evolved civilisations: the Nuraghi people in Sardinia and the Minoan culture in Thera. Both also suffered terrible natural disasters. But neither of these islands are westwards of the Straits of Gibraltar, so to accept them is to doubt Plato's geography.

Also, the advanced races on these islands disappeared about 900 years before Plato – he stated that Atlantis became extinct 9,000 years before him.

Other experts say Atlantis was in the middle of the Atlantic, and all that is left of the island are its mountains, the peaks of which show through above the waves. These are now believed by many to be the Azore islands. There is also evidence to suggest a huge comet or asteroid crashed into the southwest Atlantic Ocean many thousands of years ago and two 23,000-feet-deep holes have been identified on the seabed close to Puerto Rico. Experts believe the falling rock that caused them would have created massive natural movements, enough to destroy any mid-Atlantic islands.

El Dorado

WHEN THE CONQUISTADORS were ravaging and looting the ancient cultures of the Aztecs and Incas, native tribesmen told them about an amazing rumour. They said that there was a race, deep in the jungle, whose king was covered with gold dust and who swam in a golden lake. It was the story of 'El Dorado,' the 'Golden Man.' One of the first Spaniards to set off to find this fantasy land was Jimenez de Quesada. In 1536, Quesada and 500 soldiers hacked into the undergrowth from the northwest of what is now Columbia. After many hard days trudging through intense and dangerous jungle, they came upon two tribes of Chibchas, a race with plentiful riches. They had gold, silver and huge amounts of emeralds, but they did not have the fabled 'El Dorado.' However, they told Quesada of a lake in the middle of a huge volcanic crater on the Bogota plateau not far away.

The natives revealed that the lake was called Guatavita and each year the bizarre ceremony of the Golden Man would take place. Tribal witnesses said the occasion was used to offer sacrifices and gifts to the god that they worshipped. The tribal king was smeared in sticky mud, on which gold dust was set. He and four other chiefs then sailed on a raft with their finest jewels and treasures, whilst the tribe played music at the shoreline. When the king and his party reached the centre of the lake they threw the offerings into the water, and the king then bathed himself to remove his golden covering. Quesada travelled to the lake, but could find no clue hinting at treasure. Other Spaniards heard the rumours about Guatavita, and the first attempt to dredge the lake began in 1545.

As the years passed, each new expedition heard other versions of the El Dorado legend. Each one ploughed into the jungle certain they would find the wealth. None ever did, but they did come across other interesting things. In 1537, one adventurer, Francisco de Orellana, was trying to find the golden city by sailing down the Napo River. Orellana reached the end of the Napo, and realised it was a tributary to another, massive river. As he floated along this, a tribe of long-haired, fierce female archers attacked his boat. The women reminded Orellano of the Amazons of Scythia in Greek legend, and he named the river 'Amazonas'.

In 1584 another native rumour appeared. It suggested that Incas fleeing from the Spanish invaders had created a new city of gold called Manoa. This became inseparable from the El Dorado legend, and in 1595 the British adventurer Sir Walter Raleigh attempted to find Manoa and its gold for Queen Elizabeth I. He failed, and a further fruitless expedition in 1617 helped to seal his execution. Over the years, yet another myth circulated – that of a lost mystical lake called Parima. It was described as being almost identical to Quesada's initial discovery, Lake Guatavita. Despite this, more expeditions floundered in the jungle, haphazardly slicing their way through the foliage until they ran out of supplies, funds, men or patience.

Meanwhile, other Spaniards had decided to continue attempts at reaching the bottom of Lake Guatavita. In 1580s, Antonio de Sepulveda, a merchant living in Bogota, used

8000 native men to drain the lake by cutting a huge gash in the side. He did manage to remove a fair deal of water, and found considerable gold, but the earth walls collapsed, killing many workmen and causing the project to be abandoned. Further attempts to drain the lake continued right into the twentieth century, and many historically valuable artefacts were found, but never the great quantities of treasure promised by the legends.

There can be little doubt that, despite the countless and varied attempts hunting through the jungle, the Conquistadors never uncovered all the secrets of the Amazon. Biology, botany and anthropology show us that there is still plenty of potential for new discoveries. Did the Spanish adventurers really find the lake of El Dorado? Almost certainly Lake Guatavita is that fabled lagoon. But nobody has found yet Manoa, and if the El Dorado myth has been proven real, there is good reason to suspect the Manoan legend will be too.

LYONESSE

OFF THE VERY SOUTHWEST tip of Land's End, in Cornwall, England, there lies nothing but water and a few small islands called the Scilly Isles. Legend says that under the fierce Atlantic Ocean waves rests the remains of a beautiful old kingdom called Lyonesse. It is a kingdom steeped in the legends of King Arthur and was once overcome by a great flood. Locals believe that if you look in the right direction at low tide you can even see the submerged towers and domes. Sometimes, late at night, it is possible to hear the ghostly tolling of lost church bells.

Lyonesse is said to be a great country that contained magnificent cities and stretched to the distant west off Land's End, from St Michael's Mount to beyond the Scilly Isles. There were supposed to be 140 churches in the country, and great forests covering the area. However, on 11th November 1099 a terrible flood raged over the land, drowning all but one of the inhabitants. This single survivor was a man called Trevilian, who saw the waves coming and rode his horse to safety on higher ground. The Trevlyan coat of arms still shows a white horse rising from the sea, but the cities of Lyonesse were lost forever, and only the highest points of the kingdom peaked through the waves. At a distance of 20 miles from Land's End, we now know these summits as the Scilly Isles.

Another variation of the Lyonesse legend says that when King Arthur was wounded in his final battle against Mordred, the remnants of his foe's army chased the king to Lyonesse. As Arthur and his men reached the highest points in the kingdom, the ghost of Merlin appeared. He called the terrible flood and Mordred's forces were drowned. It is said that Arthur then died on the Scilly Isles, and the association between King Arthur and Lyonesse has been extended by imaginative minds over the years. Alfred Lord Tennyson even suggested the great king may have had his fabled, mystical court, Camelot, there.

So what proof is there to accompany these fanciful myths? To begin with, surrounding St Michael's Mount at low tide, the fossilised remains of an ancient forest can be seen. So there once was definitely woodland under

King Arthur: was he a native of the lost land of Lyonesse?

what is now sea. Similarly, at low tide around the Scilly Isles, it is also possible to spot walls and ruins running from the islands' shores. In the 1920s it was believed that structures found on the beach at Samson Flats were field boundary markers, although more recent thought considers that they were probably fish traps. But definite remains of hut circles and cysts on other islands suggests the water really has risen. Indeed, writings as late as the fourth century AD state that the Scilly Isles were one singular land mass.

A group of rocks positioned halfway between Land's End and the Scilly Isles, known as the Seven Stones, are believed to mark the site of a once great city. Sailors and local fishermen call the area 'The Town'. Some of these mariners have even reported catching parts of doors and windows in their nets around the area. In the 1930s, Stanley Baron, a journalist from the London paper, News Chronicle was staying in Sennen Cove, just north of Land's End, when he was awoken one night by the sound of muffled bells. His hosts explained that he had heard the ghostly tolling of Lyonesse's churches. Another reliable witness, Edith Oliver, was a former mayor of the town of Wilton in Salisbury. She claimed to have twice seen the towers, spires and domes of Lyonesse emerging from the waves as she looked out from Land's End.

Science, however, refuses to accept these legends. Oceanographers are convinced that in the last 3,000 years there has not been a big enough change in tidal height to account for any of these phenomena. But even if they disprove the fantastical stories, there is still real evidence at the shore edge on many of the Scilly Isles. And anyway, oceanographic proof alone is not enough to dissuade old Cornish seadogs. Sometimes a story is so magical it seems silly to let science spoil it.

MU AND LEMURIA

ANCIENT LEGENDS TELL of a great continent now lost under the sea. Sanskrit tradition calls the continent 'Rutas' and says that it sank under the Indian Ocean. Tamil writings recorded on palm tree bark tell of a giant land mass that connected southern India to Australia. All across the islands of the Pacific Ocean there are legends of a massive continent that was the birthplace of Man and which sank under the waves. This lost land we now refer to as 'Mu' or 'Lemuria'.

James Churchward, an Anglo-American traveller, wrote the first accounts of Mu legend. He said he was taught Mankind's original tongue, a dialect called 'Naacal,' by an Indian priest. This holy man then showed him some old stone tablets hidden in a temple, written in this ancient language. These tablets explained that Mu was a continent in the Pacific Ocean. Placed just below the equator, it was 5,000 miles long and 3,000 miles wide. The tablets said that

Mankind had appeared on Mu two million years ago, and a highly advanced society of 64 million people had developed on the island before they were all but wiped out by a huge volcanic eruption.

Around the same time as Churchward was publicising his legend and tradition-based theory, another more scientific group were advancing the idea of a lost land. Naturalists and zoologists who followed and believed Charles Darwin's theory of evolution were finding it particularly difficult to explain the widespread existence of lemurs. If these animals had all descended from a common ancestor, as Darwin suggested, then there

must have once been a land link between these areas. One of Darwin's followers, an English zoologist called Philip L. Schlater, proposed the name 'Lemuria' for this invented sunken land bridge.

As science has progressed since Darwin's time, zoologists can now account for the wide distribution of the lemur family without resorting to creating ideas of ancient missing land masses. But at the same time, genetic discoveries have proven that, because of a massive natural catastrophe that almost induced human extinction, all of Mankind originally stems from a small pool of biological variations.

TEOTIHAUCÁN

HIGH ON A PLATEAU in central Mexico lies the remains of a city that continues to perplex archaeologists and historians. Of all the ancient cities of the Americas, Teotihaucán is the most enigmatic. Nobody knows what race of people built it, what they used it for, or why it was abandoned. Indeed, the remains are awe-inspiring, but it is believed that 90% of the city is still buried under the arid Mexican soil. And yet, this great city of culture held 200,000 inhabitants at its peak. So what happened at Teotihaucán?

When later Aztec races found this amazing urban development they were so impressed by its construction that they named it 'Teotihaucán,' meaning 'The great city where men become gods.' The focal point of the city, which spread over 12 square miles, was an immense building called the Pyramid of the Sun. This 216-feet-tall structure had a temple at its summit which indicated the

city was ruled by native religion. At the base of the pyramid ran a north-south avenue, which stretched for almost three miles. The Aztecs called this the 'Avenue of the Dead,' believing the small platforms that lined the series of connecting courtyards to be tombs. In fact, they were probably temples – it has since been discovered that the Teotihaucáns actually buried the dead in their own houses.

At the northern end of the 'avenue,' nearest the Sun Pyramid, there was a slightly smaller construction, named the Pyramid of the Moon. About a mile south down the avenue there was a vast open area called the Citadel. This was also surrounded by temples and had the important Temple of the Feathered Serpent in its centre. Intersecting the Avenue of the Dead at its halfway point was another avenue. The city was therefore based on a grid system of four quarters. The houses in this format were built in complexes of adjoining dwellings, linked by

The great Sun Pyramid of Teotihaucán rises above a plateau in Mexico.

terraces and patios. The building of the city began around 200BC, with the major structures, like the pyramids, being erected from the first century AD. By the beginning of the fifth century AD, the city covered its maximum surface area, and housed around 100,000 people. Within two centuries this number had doubled.

But who were the inhabitants? Archaeologists and historians really do not know for certain. They were much too early to be Aztecs, and the Toltec race, despite having a similar sense of architecture and civil engineering, did not appear until 200 years after the initial building of Teotihuacán. There is a possibility that the Olmecs, a race of great builders and craftsmen who had flourished between the fifteenth century BC and first century AD, may have been their ancestors. However, there is no proof to confirm this, and the writings and records left by the Teotihaucáns, which would provide us with their own version of their history, have never been successfully translated to. Whoever founded the city did so with intelligent laws and a strict reverence to religious matters. It has been suggested that the city was a major destination for pilgrims and the training centre for priests.

Despite the people enjoying a structured, dignified and privileged life, the city of Teotihaucán was largely destroyed by the eighth century AD. One theory is that the population may have been too great for the local resources although this has been countered by the knowledge that the rulers of Teotihaucán were good enough social and civil engineers to provide for this. It is more likely that invading barbarians from the north attacked the city. Indeed, what historians have garnered from Teotihaucán murals suggests the roles of soldiers took on more prominence in the city's later years. Teotihaucán itself was not designed to repel attacks, and recent excavations have indicated that large, prepared fires were started in the city during its last days.

Although the origin of the Teotihaucán race is unknown, the influence it had across the Mexican region has been proven to be immense. Some experts consider the possibility that a mass exodus of Teotihaucán citizens founded another town with structure similar to the earlier pyramids at a site 700 miles away in Kaminaljuyú. But nothing is known for certain. Even after nearly a century of intense historical investigation, the mysterious story of Teotihaucán is as unknown now as it has been for a thousand years.

They came, they created, they left in silence: who were the builders of Teotihaucán?

HORRORS AND
HAUNTINGS

AMITYVILLE

THE MOST FAMOUS and horrific ghost story of the last century must be that of 112 Ocean Avenue, in Amityville, New York. The terrifying tale has been turned into a best-selling book and successful film, and captured the public's attention like no other haunting. Indeed, such is its place in the American consciousness that most people assume that it is a real story – and that is certainly how it was publicised. There is no doubt that some awful events did take place in the building, but were they really caused by ghostly actions?

The now infamous three-storey Dutch colonial house was built in 1924. The owners lived happily in the building for many years, raising a family and leaving the house to their daughter who had such fond memories of her childhood home that she moved her own family into it. In 1960 the building left the care of the original owners' descendants and was bought by a couple who lived in the house until they sold it following their divorce in 1965.

In June 1965 the DeFeo family bought the house. They were an unhappy family and the father, Ronald DeFeo Sr., was known to be abusive. Over a period of nine years the family was not said to experience any type of frightening event other than those inflicted by paternal forces. However that all changed on the night of the 18th of November 1974 when one son, Ronald DeFeo Jr., shot and killed his mother, father, two brothers and two sisters.

Just over a year later, in December 1975, a young couple bought the house. George and Kathy Lutz, and her three children moved in,

George and Kathy Lutz: victims of supernatural horror, or common swindlers?

knowing the building's terrible history. Almost immediately they began experiencing strange phenomena. Doors and windows would open by themselves, bizarre noises were heard, and a Catholic priest who had come to exorcise the house was ordered to get out by a devilish voice.

Things rapidly grew worse. Blood and sticky goo oozed from the walls, clouds of flies appeared on windows, ghostly hooded apparitions manifested, and one of the children started communicating with a demonic pig called Jodie. One night Kathy Lutz was even thrown from her bed by a supernatural force, and it was famously claimed that the face of the devil appeared in the brickwork of the fireplace.

After 28 days of this horror, the Lutzes moved out. They soon went to the media with their story. In February 1976 two of America's most famous celebrity paranormal investigators, Ed and Lorraine Warren, were filmed by a television news team whilst conducting séances at the house. The Warrens stated the house was indeed haunted with evil spirits, but other investigators were not convinced.

Dr Stephen Kaplan, the executive director of the Parapsychology Institute of America, based in New York, initially had great doubts about the story, and discovered some very interesting facts about the Lutzes. However, his studies were ignored, and it transpired that the couple had already collaborated with an author, Jay Anson, and had written a book, 'The Amityville Horror – A True Story.' An instant best-seller on its release in 1977, a blockbusting movie version of the tale was released in 1979.

As Kaplan suspected, there were some dubious actions and motives behind the Amityville tale. It was revealed that Ronald DeFeo Jr's defence lawyer had met with the Lutzes before their story was released. Kaplan found no evidence to support many of the claims written in their book, but he did discover that the Lutzes were able to return to the house to hold a garage sale only a couple of weeks after apparently fleeing in terror. Similarly, many investigators noticed that the Lutzes were holding contracts for book and film rights as soon as they decided to publicise their account.

Since the Lutzes left, three different families have lived in the house with no reports of ghostly experiences. Dr Stephen Kaplan's in-depth report and its subsequent revelations about the house were never viewed with as much interest as the dramatic original story, but his book, 'The Amityville Horror Conspiracy,' was eventually published some years after his death. Many investigators and cynics have been led to conclude that the whole case really revolved around money, rather than the popular perception of paranormal influences. It seems the evil forces in this story have less to do with supernatural unknowns, and more with all too common, base human instincts.

THE BORLEY RECTORY

MANY PEOPLE BELIEVE Borley's ghostly problems began centuries ago. In 1362 Benedictine monks built a monastery in the little village in Essex, south east England. Local legend says that a monk tried to run away with a nun from the nearby Bures nunnery. Despite having an escape plan organised and a carriage ready to smuggle them away to safety, the two lovers were caught. The monk was hanged, and the nun was bricked up in the walls of the monastery's cellars.

The modern legend began in 1862, when Reverend Henry Bull became rector of Borley and built the rectory a year later in 1863. Villagers knew of the mournful nun who

Excavations at Borley Rectory.

could be seen, walking sadly round the land near the old monastery – and it seems Reverend Bull grew accustomed to her too. In 1875 he added a new wing to the rectory overlooking what was known in the village as the 'Nun's Walk' so that he could watch the ghost. However, the nun eventually became an annoyance, particularly as she had a habit of staring in the windows of the rectory, scaring many visitors.

Henry Bull died in May 1892 in the Blue Room of the rectory. His son Harry took over the building and, if anything, the tales of haunted happenings increased. Four of Henry's sisters saw the nun walking along her path, and in addition to the nun apparition, there were new sightings of a ghostly coach and horses arriving in the rectory drive. Harry Bull died in June 1927, also in the Blue Room; before his death he is claimed to have said he had experienced 'communications with spirits,' but his passing marked the end of the Bulls' physical, earthly tenancy with the rectory.

In October 1928 the Reverend Guy Eric Smith and his wife took over residency of the rectory. The Smiths knew about the house's history and soon began experiencing their own strange phenomena. Objects were moved around the house, lights were switched on and off, stones were thrown, there was even the sound of strange whispers mentioning Henry Bull's nickname – Carlos. The Smiths finally wrote to the Daily Mirror for help, and the paper dispatched the paranormal investigator, Harry Price, to the rectory.

Price recorded incidents of many unusual activities including inexplicable bell ringing and the strange appearance of a Catholic medallion. The Smiths moved out of the building and then left Borley altogether in April 1930, but the October of that year saw the start of a period Harry Price would refer to as 'the most extraordinary and best documented case of haunting in the annals of psychical research.' Reverend Lionel Foyster, his young wife Marianne and their adopted daughter Adelaide moved into the rectory and immediately the phenomena worsened.

Marianne faced the worst of the poltergeist attacks – objects were thrown at her, and messages addressed to her appeared scribbled across the walls. One message read, 'Marianne, please help get. Pleas for help and prayers.' The Reverend Foyster decided to have the rectory exorcised and things settled down for a short time, although the hauntings returned and Marianne was repeatedly thrown from her bed by spiritual forces. Reverend Foyster finally decided to move his family away from the area, and all subsequent rectors have refused to live in the house.

By June 1937 Harry Price himself decided to rent the building and installed a team of observers. On 27th March 1938 a séance was held in the rectory. A spirit voice said the rectory would catch fire in the hallway, that very night and burn down. It did not. Price's tenancy expired and the house was taken over by Captain William Gregson and his wife. On 27th February 1939 Captain Gregson was in his library when a lamp in the hallway fell over. Eleven months later than the spirits warned, Borley Rectory burnt to the ground. Witnesses saw strange apparitions dancing in the flames, and the nun's face was said to be seen staring from an upper window.

Before the rectory was razed in 1944, Price returned to the site and was hunting in the cellars when he found the jawbone of a young woman. He believed it belonged to the infamous nun, and gave it a Christian burial. However, it has not stopped the strange occurrences and many locals now believe the spirits inhabit the Borley church and churchyard across the road.

HAMPTON COURT PALACE

HAMPTON COURT PALACE on the banks of the River Thames, just outside London, is said to be the most haunted royal building in Britain. Most palaces and castles are known to house a few mythical spectres, but the special quality about Hampton Court is the sheer range of apparitions. From wives of King Henry VIII, to Cavalier soldiers, to a ghostly dog, the palace is plagued by over a dozen unexplained phenomena.

Hampton Court was originally bought by Cardinal Wolsey, but Henry VIII liked the building and took it as his own. Henry was the first person to report seeing the decapitated head of his second wife, Anne Boleyn who was executed for treasonous adultery in 1536. Subsequent sightings of her have described her with, without and even carrying her head. Witnesses say she appears in blue or black, walking slowly, looking angry or upset, and is said to pervade a sense of grief or despair.

Henry's third wife, Jane Seymour, reportedly the love of his life, was the only wife to be buried alongside him in his death vault.

Hampton Court Palace, site of many ghostly sightings, usually of one or other of Henry VIII's unfortunate wives.

She died giving birth to his only son, Edward, in 1537 and was the only one of his queens to die of natural causes before Henry. It is said that on the anniversary of Edward's birth, 12th October, Lady Jane appears from the Queen's Apartments and walks round to the Silver Stick Gallery. Witnesses say the apparition wears a white robe and carries a lit candle.

With Jane's death, Henry's new-born son was entrusted to the care of a nursemaid, Sibell Penn. Penn died of smallpox in 1562 and was buried in St Mary's Church, not far from the palace in Hampton. Her spirit was not seen or heard from until the 1820s when St Mary's Church was stuck by lightning and during the rebuilding, Penn's remains were removed to another grave.

Since then there have been reports of a tall, hooded figure known as the 'Grey Lady' walking the corridors of the palace at the same time as a strange spinning noise was heard in the west wing of the building. The whirring sound seemed to be coming from an odd wall of a corridor, so during investigations the wall was knocked down. Behind it they found a previously unknown room, along with Sibell Penn's old spinning wheel.

Undoubtedly the most celebrated ghost in Hampton Court can be found in what is called the Haunted Gallery. The ghost is that of Henry's fifth wife, Catherine Howard, who was beheaded in 1542 for infidelity with younger men. Legend has it that the moments following the ordering of her execution can be seen played out by spectres in the gallery. Witnesses say Catherine's figure appears screaming for her life, until guards seize her and drag her away. Some people have also seen her trying to find sanctuary in the palace chapel, whilst a palace warder once reported seeing a ghostly hand wearing one of Catherine's heavily jewelled rings knocking on the chapel door.

Not all the restless spirits that wander the hallways of the palace are of royal lineage. Palace staff have seen a strange grey mist floating along the kitchen floor, and a guard reported seeing a dark, male figure wearing a top hat who just disappeared in the wine cellar. (Witnesses said it was strange, as he looked more like a spirit man!) There are also tales of a ghostly dog being seen entering the King's Apartments.

Many people have reported seeing two noisy figures fighting in the main courtyard. During renovation work in the yard, the skeletons of two English Civil War Cavalier soldiers were found and given a proper burial. There have been no sightings of the figures since. A group of seven women and two men dressed in old-fashioned clothing are also said to wander Hampton Court. In 1917 a police officer even opened a door for these apparitions, before they simply disappeared into thin air.

Nowadays, visitors to the palace should not be concerned if they see some strange characters in period dress, for many of the specialist guides giving tours of the building now appear in costume. If people do see a ghost there, it seems that none of them are harmful. That said, one lady warder at the palace was standing on duty when she felt something flick her underwear elastic. Perhaps the spirit of Henry is lurking somewhere – and it would seem entirely possible that he has not changed his ways.

LONGENDALE GHOSTPLANES

THE PEAK DISTRICT is an area of sombre, imposing natural beauty between Manchester and Sheffield in the north of England. Britain's first National Park, it is still the most visited National Park in Europe. It can be a dark, doleful place; a place where tradition and legend come alive; where history blurs with the present and where things can sometimes happen with no obvious explanation. In the west of the Peaks, running towards Manchester, lies the Longendale Valley. It is not only attracts tourists and leisure-seekers, but is also one of Britain's most active sites for UFO enthusiasts and ghost-hunters. However, Longendale has one particularly unique type of supernatural story – Ghostplanes.

The area has a long association with aircraft. The reservoirs in the area were used by the 'Dambusters' squadron to test their bouncing bombs during the Second World War. Although these tests saw no fatal accidents, there have been over 50 cases where planes have found themselves lost in fog and crashed into the moors. In all, over three hundred airmen have died in these accidents. There is also a remarkable range of tales from people witnessing phantom vintage aircraft seemingly in trouble. It is such a common occurrence that the local park rangers and mountain rescue teams have almost become used to being called out for plane crashes that they cannot find.

A striking recent example happened on the night of 24th March 1990. Many people were in the Peaks away from the city lights to watch the passing Hale-Bopp comet when they saw a large, low flying aircraft, like an old Lancaster bomber, on a collision course with local hills. Emergency switchboards lit up with a series of calls reporting the accident, with a staggering number of reliable witnesses. Two of them were Marie-Frances Tattersfield, a police special constable, and her husband, a former pilot.

Mrs Tattersfield said the plane was 'The weirdest thing I have ever seen... it was big and it was well below the legal altitude for night flying. All its windows were lit up which made it look even more odd as no pilot would fly blind at that time of night over those hills.' The police launched a search and rescue operation with over a hundred volunteers, but no trace of any plane or crash was spotted.

But the remains of many stricken aircraft do still litter the hills of the area. On one,

called Bleaklow, lies the shattered carcass of a B-29 Superfortress that crashed on 3rd November 1948, killing all 13 crew. Local children who play on the hill tell stories of a man in uniform who revealed he is guardian of the site. They say he told them about the history of the aircraft and its crew, before vanishing. When shown photos of the dead aircrew, the children have been shocked to find the man they met was the doomed plane's captain, Langdon P. Tanner.

It is not just children that have seen the captain. Gerald Scarratt witnessed the B-29 crash as a boy, but only visited the site two decades later. He investigated around the remains of the wreckage and found a gold ring engraved with the name 'Langdon P. Tanner.' Soon after hearing of his discovery, a group of aircraft enthusiasts asked if he could take them to the wreck, 'I bent down to show them where I found the ring, and when I looked up they had scarpered and were ten or fifteen yards away.

'When I caught up with them they were ashen-faced. They said they had seen someone standing behind me, looking down and dressed in full flying uniform. I told them I had seen nothing, but they said: 'We've all seen him, thanks for taking us up, but we are going.' And I have never seen or heard from them again,' Scarratt said.

It would seem that, whether flying through the skies, or buried in the earth, there are some things in the Peak District which are beyond the realm of the explainable.

THE MARY CELESTE

THE TALE OF THE 'Mary Celeste' is not technically a ghost story, but thanks to one of the finest fiction writers of all time the true story of this ship has passed into legend as one of the most perplexing of naval mysteries. It was Sir Arthur Conan Doyle who, as a young writer, was commissioned to pen a tale about a vessel that had been found wandering across the Atlantic Ocean in perfect condition but completely crewless. He changed the name slightly, calling it the 'Marie Celeste,' and added fictional embellishments. But the facts themselves are strange enough and, to this day, nobody quite knows what happened to those aboard the 'Mary Celeste.'

Originally called the 'Amazon,' the ship was built in Nova Scotia in 1860. She was a 100 foot long, 282 tonne brigantine or half-brig. Right from the start she was an unlucky ship: she suffered numerous accidents and ended up in a dire state of repair at a New York salvage auction in 1868. The three new owners, James H. Winchester, Silvester Godwin and Benjamin Spooner Briggs, repaired and refitted the 'Amazon.' They registered her in New York under the name 'Mary Celeste.'

Having been the master on three previous ships, Briggs took on the role as captain. Viewed as an honest, upright, God-fearing man, he was a captain who would only abandon his ship in the most appalling conditions. On 7th November 1872 the 'Mary Celeste' left New York with Briggs, his wife Sarah, their daughter Sophie Matilda, and a crew of seven. Their cargo was 1700 barrels of American alcohol bound for Genoa in Italy.

A week later the British frigatine the 'Dei Gratia' left America to follow a similar route across the Atlantic. Captain David Reed Morehouse, who had dined with Briggs only a few days before the 'Mary Celeste' left port, ran the 'Dei Gratia.' On 4th December the 'Dei Gratia' was 400 miles east of the Azores when its crew spotted a ship sailing haphazardly ahead of them. Through his spyglass, Morehouse could see it was the 'Mary Celeste.' As there was no sign of activity on deck, and no reply came to any attempt at hailing her, Morehouse decided to send off a boarding party.

Chief Mate of the 'Dei Gratis,' Oliver Deveau, was dispatched as leader of the group who set off in a small boat. He found the ship in a perfectly sailable condition with good supplies of food and water, but with a certain amount of interior damage. There was a great deal of water over the ship's decks, and one of the pumps was broken. The galley stove had moved from its correct position, and the ship's clock and compass were also damaged.

The crew appeared to have left quickly, as their waterproof boots and pipes were still on board, but it looked as though Captain Briggs had taken the chronometer and sextant. Deveau noticed that there were no lifeboats left on the ship. The most interesting find was the ship's log. The last entry was dated 24th November, when the

Clipper ship similar to the *Mary Celeste.*

'Mary Celeste' was only just passing the Azores. That meant the ship had sailed itself for over 400 miles on a perfectly-plotted course for the Mediterranean.

The crew of the 'Dei Gratia' now split into two groups. One stayed on their own ship, whilst the other sailed the 'Mary Celeste' onto Gibraltar. The cargo of alcohol reached Genoa with only nine barrels damaged. Following a naval inquiry, the 'Mary Celeste' was sold on and then continued to change hands frequently. After hearing her history, many mariners decided that she was not the sort of ship they were too keen on. In 1884 she was wrecked off the coast of Haiti in an alleged insurance scam. But what happened to her crew in 1872?

The official version of events, arrived at by the British and American authorities, was that the crew had mutinied and then abandoned ship. This seems very unlikely as it was only a short journey and there were no signs of a struggle on board. Also, Briggs was generally viewed as a decent and respected captain.

A second theory is almost completely implausible. It came from a man called Fosdyk who left papers after his death saying he was a secret passenger on the 'Mary Celeste.' He claimed that Briggs had constructed a special deck in the bow for his daughter. During the voyage, two of the crew were having a swimming race around the boat when one man was attacked by sharks. As the rest of the ship's passengers crowded onto the little girl's deck to see what was happening, the temporary structure gave way, sending all those on board into the sea and to the sharks. Fosdyk claimed to have survived by clinging to a piece of driftwood.

The most probable explanation, given the facts, was that the 'Mary Celeste' hit a terrible patch of bad weather. As the ship bucked on the waves, some alcohol spilled from the cargo barrels, covering the hold floor. Coupled with this, the ship's movement caused the galley stove to become unstable. Fearing the ship was about to explode, Briggs ordered everybody into the lifeboat, and planned to follow behind the 'Mary Celeste' attached to the ship's main halyard, a strong, thick rope.

As the storm worsened, somehow the halyard snapped and the 'Mary Celeste' sailed off. Briggs, his family and crew were left stranded in a small boat in the middle of the Atlantic Ocean. There is some evidence for this scenario. Morehouse testified that the 'Dei Gratia' had been battered in severe storms during the days leading up to finding the 'Mary Celeste.' As mentioned earlier, Deveau noticed alcohol and water spilled over the boards of the ship, whilst the galley and its stove were found in a very disorderly condition. Crucially, Deveau also noted that all small boats were missing, and the halyard was found dangling, frayed and split, over the side of the ship.

Ghost ships were not particularly rare during the nineteenth century. The Dutch schooner 'Hermania' and the ship 'Marathon' were both found abandoned but floating in perfect order around the same time as the 'Mary Celeste.' However, with the help of Conan Doyle, it was the 'Mary Celeste' that really caught the public's interest. Whilst his, and our, imagination can come up with possibilities, the true fate of the souls aboard the 'Mary Celeste' is something we will probably never know.

WATERWORKS VALLEY

WATERWORKS VALLEY, in the parish of St Lawrence in the Channel Island of Jersey, is named after the great number of reservoirs and pumping stations found along it. Even in the daytime, it is a brooding, haunting place, overcast as it is by a thick layer of trees and foliage. It is damp and dark, and people are often forgiven for seeing or hearing things. Sometimes there is no mistaking the ghostly sights and sounds that occur. Countless people have seen it pass by, and even more have run away after hearing it approach. This, they say, is the 'Phantom Carriage.'

The stories often follow a similar pattern. Usually the events occur in the evening and begin with the muffled ringing of bells – the unearthly music is said to sound more like wedding bells than anything sombre. Gradually, mixed with ringing, another noise becomes discernible. It is the sound of horses trotting along the valley, accompanied by the spinning, bumping rattles of a carriage. Emerging from the gloom, witnesses spot the procession which is clothed in eighteenth century costume. They see that the coach's passenger is a bride in her wedding dress, but as it rolls past witnesses see the face behind the veil. It is the haggard skull of a corpse.

One tale of explanation claims that in the early eighteenth century a girl who was due to be married at St Lawrence parish church was disappointed at the altar. It is said she committed suicide that evening, and the apparition is a representation of her timeless sorrow. Another variation of the story is that she committed suicide on the eve of the wedding, but her ghostly figure appeared at the church the next day anyway. It was only as the groom lifted the veil that he noticed the pale lifeless face of a corpse underneath. Many people believe the phenomenon happens only once a year at a specific time. But there are so many sightings, and such vivid recollections, that perhaps this poor girl's misery is constant and never-ending.

MARVELS AND MIRACLES

Angels

THE IDEA THAT angels exist is not solely the intellectual belief of the Roman Catholic Church. Many people of all religions have experienced feelings or events that instilled a belief that something is watching over them, protecting them. Whether that is a divine being depends on the person's own belief in God. There is also a case for saying that many people feel guided by a guardian angel, which does not have to be a religious entity, but can be a deceased relative or friend. In both cases, the angel's role is to give warning of impending danger, and comfort in times of difficulty. Their effect on an individual's life can be immense.

One fascinating story concerns Sergei Kourdakov who, as a Russian KGB agent, was instructed not to believe deity-based faiths. Indeed, Kourdakov was in a squad purposely set up to persecute and intimidate Christian groups. On one occasion, he claims his team raided a secret Bible meeting with the task of punishing those present. Kourdakov noticed an old woman standing in the corner holding her Bible. He went over to beat her, but as he pulled his arm back to punch her, some strange presence held it behind him. He turned round but there was nobody there. Eventually, Kourdakov ended up defecting to the United States.

The religious view of angels is that they are solely God's messengers. They appear to give news of great events – for example, telling the shepherds of Christ's birth. Their role is to perform God's commands and reveal the most important truths to Man.

Lucifer falls from Heaven in this nineteenth century engraving.

Often they instil awe in those that see them, but they are said to exude a calm confidence. Although they feature regularly throughout both the Old and New Testament, it is not just bible-based religions that experience the phenomenon. Diverse races and cultures have all recorded startlingly similar accounts of meetings with mystical creatures, and they are often associated with miracles and inexplicable healing powers.

Angels in chariots descend to earth. Theologians have struggled to classify the different classes of angel for centuries.

BIBLE CODE

THE IDEA OF Bible Codes began in the twelfth century when Jewish students discovered interesting and relevant hidden words in the Hebrew version of the Torah, the first five books of the Bible. Devout Jews believe that details of everything that will ever happen on Earth are recorded here; the great Rabbis have always stressed that as these writings were dictated by Moses straight from God, no alterations should be made to the text.

The modern era of Bible Codes was begun by Michael Ber Weissmandl – a Slovakian rabbi who narrowly escaped the Nazi death chambers. His interest in ancient books about Bible Codes led him to develop his own theories. Although the Second World War had helped to ruin Weissmandl's old life, it did promote the idea of code-breakers, with the famous stories of the German Enigma programme. It also marked the beginning of micro-computers, and many Torah scholars, fascinated by Weissmandl's ideas, were able to harness complex technology to further the research into Bible Codes.

In 1994 a group of intellects, Doron Witztum, Eliyahu Rips and Yoav Rosenberg, published a study in the Statistical Science journal of an experiment they had conducted using methods developed by Weissmandl. They said they had found references to 34 Great Rabbi Sages, together with their respective birth and death dates, hidden in the book of Genesis. This study ignited the scientific and popular interest in Bible Codes, which is still active today, and has led to many more books being produced, although not all of these have had such groundings in scientific procedures.

So how are the messages in the Bible decoded? In its simplest form, the research uses a system called Equidistant Letter Sequencing. This works by placing all the letters in the text next to each other, with no spaces or punctuation. Then, by performing uniform jumps along the letter chain, other words are discernible. For example:

ARETHEREHIDDENMESSAGESHERE

In the above passage, by skipping to every sixth letter from the starting point, we get the word 'ties.' The method can be used forwards or backwards, with any number of letter jumping or spacing. There are even more complicated ways of decoding, called arrays or matrices; they are a two dimensional presentation of the text – rather like a word search puzzle – which contain hidden words in different directions.

Weissmandl's initial discovery was that by taking the first T in the first verse of the book of Genesis, and then skipping 50 letters three times you end up with the word TVRH, the Hebrew spelling of Torah. This finding applies with the same 50 letter skips in the first verses in the book of Exodus and Numbers. More recent research has shown

GHTE**R**STH**O**UHA**S**TNO**W**DONE**E**FOO**L**ISH**L**YINS

"Roswell" hidden in KJV Genisis 31:28

references to Hitler, 'Mein Kampf,' and other historical events. However, sensationalist authors have rather corrupted the system to produce fanciful assertions, and the Bible Code has become a phenomenon rather akin to the prophecies of Nostradamus. Subsequently some researchers have tried to use it as a method of foretelling the future.

Many Code enthusiasts believe it is not supposed to be seen as a way of deducing our fate, but should be seen as proof that the Torah was actually written by God, who had knowledge of all that would come to pass. They say that searching the text for references to future events that might occur is not valid, because if they fail to happen, then they would just be random word formations. Many people believe the valid details that do seem to appear in the Bible Code are merely random words which just happen to correspond to a real event.

Certainly, there is a huge body of sceptical statistical and computer experts in the scientific world. Two such intellectuals, mathematicians Dror Bar-Natan and Brendan McKay, were the first to refute the findings of Witztum, Rips and Rosenberg. McKay and Bar-Natan found similar results when looking for the details of famous Rabbis within the text of Tolstoy's War and Peace. Other experiments have also revealed a foretelling of famous assassinations, Princess Diana's death and the 'War on Terrorism' all hidden in the text of Melville's Moby Dick.

The Bible Code breakers say they are pursuing this subject to prove God actually did write the Bible although one is tempted to think that an overly elaborate code system will have little effect on the faith of either a believer or an atheist.

THE BIG BANG

THE GREATEST, MOST fundamental mystery in the history of the world and the universe is; how did this all begin? Man now knows a lot about the different stages of Earth's development, but he still has no definite answers for how our world came to be here or even how the universe came to be formed. Religion provides us with one theory – the idea that God created the planets by hand, but that does not tally with the few pieces of scientific evidence that we do possess. For, although we are still largely ignorant, science has begun to reveal some of the secrets of the cosmos. We do not know much, but we do know it all started with a bang. A Big Bang.

About 15 billion years ago there was an enormous explosion. Incredible, trillion-degree heat, matter and anti-matter were created in a dense expanding cloud. In less than 1000th of a second, the universe had doubled in size over 100 times. More matter than anti-matter was produced, and basic particles began to form. The universe remained a thick, plasmatic substance, made up mainly of radiation at an extreme, but cooling, heat. After a second, the universe had a temperature of ten billion degrees Kelvin. The process continued, with simple particles gradually slowing in speed, allowing for more complex reactions to take place.

About three minutes after the initial explosion, the temperature was down to a billion degrees. Nucleosynthesis was beginning to take place, and deuterium, an isotope known as heavy hydrogen, was being created. Deuterium then formed into tritium, which then became a helium nucleus. With slightly more cooling, hydrogen atoms were created. Over the next 300,000 years, helium atoms were formed, and the universe dropped to a temperature of 10,000 degrees Celcius as it expanded. Radiation gradually became less dense and it, light and matter were able to separate. Eventually, after 15 billion years, the universe became what we know today.

Although the Big Bang theory is based on the guesswork of many eminent cosmologists and astronomers, it is supported by a scientific basis. Recent discoveries have also helped to provide proof. NASA's COBE satellite has detected cosmic microwaves produced at the distant edges of the universe. The fact that these microwaves followed a similar rigid structure suggested the universe developed in a verifiable pattern. Slight temperature differences at three far-off points have also helped to prove scientists' earlier theories about what happened as the cosmos cooled. The different stages in development between areas of different heat give a good indication of what happened following the Big Bang.

In June 1995, scientists working on NASA's Astro-2 observatory were able to detect deuterium in the distant corners of the cosmos. This suggests such elements really did exist soon after the Big Bang. Similarly, the Hubble telescope has allowed astronomers to look deep into the universe and discover what substances are predominant in older features. These new discoveries often lead to new questions, and reworkings of old theories. What we can be certain of is that the universe continues to expand, so the Big Bang phenomenon is still in progress. The

Research into the origins of the universe currently supports the Big Bang theory.

fact that these procedures are still in effect at the far reaches of the universe provides hope that, as our observational techniques improve, we will definitely be able to learn how the universe initially expanded

As an intelligent life form, we may feel confident enough to scientifically state the conditions at the very dawn of time and space. However, no scientist would dare to suggest exactly what existed before the Big Bang. Religious philosophers have stated that everything has a cause, and have used our ignorance of the subject as proof of God. Others state that not all happenings necessarily have a catalyst, and as we are entering a completely new realm of the unknown, the normal rules of the universe may not apply.

In either case, it is a subject for philosophy, rather than physics or chemistry. What science can say is that everything around us is made up of particles that burst from an origin smaller than an atom, 15 billion years ago. Anything else remains a mystery.

THE CHILDREN OF FATIMA

ON 13TH MAY 2001, a frail, tired Pope John Paul II finished the final leg of his own personal pilgrimage. He had travelled to the little town of Adjustrel, near Fatima in Portugal. His aim was to beatify the life of two children who had died over 80 years previously. They were two of the three 'Children of Fatima,' who had been repeatedly visited by the spirit of the Virgin Mary in 1917. The holy vision had told them three prophecies, which the children kept secret, only ever revealing them to subsequent Popes. Over the years, the Roman Catholic Church explained that all but the final prediction had come to pass. But, as the Pope paid homage to the children,

he finally revealed the details of the third secret – it was a warning that saved his life.

On 13th May 1917, three children were tending their sheep at the Cova da Iria, near the town of Fatima. The two youngest children, nine-year-old Francisco and seven-year-old Jacinto Marto were brother and sister. They were helping their cousin, ten-year-old Lucia de Jesus, with her flock. All were good children, coming from strong Catholic families. They would recite the Rosary each midday without fail, and then continue with their work or play. On this occasion, a flash interrupted their afternoon activities. They though it was lightning, so they turned to leave for home, but were stopped by a beautiful lady dressed in a white robe that shone brighter than the sun. The lady had a Rosary hanging from her palm, and she instructed the children to come back and visit the site on the 13th day of each of the next five months.

The children returned as they were told. Over the following months the lady told them three secrets about future events, and promised them a miracle by their last meeting. The story of the vision spread, and a crowd of 70,000 spectators came to the site to the see the final vision on 13th October, although the lady only appeared to the children. She told them she was 'Our Lady of the Rosary' and asked them to build a chapel on the site of the visions. She then performed her miracle, which was experienced by the entire crowd. They called it the 'Miracle of the Sun' because the huge glowing orb seemed to burst into a magnificent array of colours, dancing around the skies, and the heavens rained flowers.

The children had also received visions of their own deaths. For Francisco and Jacinta,

they did not have to wait long. They both died of pneumonia, Francisco in April 1919 and his sister in February 1920. Although they were both initially buried at the Fatima parish cemetery, their remains were removed and placed in the Chapel of the Apparitions, built on the Cova de Iria site. Lucia de Jesus took holy orders after seeing the visions and became a nun. In the 1940s she sent a letter to Pope Pius XII, written in Portuguese, describing the visions.

The first secret was a vision of Hell and salvation, which the Vatican understood to be a prediction of the Second World War. The second prophecy was the rise and fall of Communism. The third secret was kept from the public. Many theories suggested it revealed the end of the world, but during the Pope's visit to Fatima in 2001, his officials revealed it was actually a vision of a white-robed priest falling to the ground. The Pope interpreted this as a forewarning of the assassination attempt on him in St Peter's Square, Rome on, amazingly, 13th May 1981.

The Pontiff believes the Virgin Mary steered the bullets away from causing mortal death, and helped him survive. He is so convinced of the role of the Fatima visions in his recovery that one of the bullets fired during the attack has been placed in the crown of the statue of the Virgin Mary at the Chapel of the Apparitions. This episode brought to end one of this century's most mysterious tales of the Roman Catholic Church. It seems strange that the mystery was really caused by the Vatican's secrecy, whereas the supernatural miracles involved are openly known and accepted. As so often happens in religion, the actions of men in response are often more confusing than the original inexplicable event.

The Angel of Fatima; did she really foretell the assassination attempt on the Pope on 13 May 1981?

DEAD SEA SCROLLS

THE NORTHERN SHORE of the Dead Sea is a parti cularly dry, arid place. It is 13 miles from Jerusalem, and even though the area is often shrouded in haze, the humidity levels are extremely low: it is the perfect place to preserve ancient artefacts. In the spring of 1947 two young Bedouin shepherds were looking for a lost goat among the cliffs in the area known as Qumran. As they hunted from cave to cave, they came upon a store of jars containing many papyrus and parchment manuscripts. These scrolls only came to prominence later that year when the Bedouin sold seven of the texts to a local antiquities dealer. As the academic world grew to hear about the discoveries, intense excitement burst through the global community of historians. Little did they know that this would be the most important discovery of ancient scrolls in the entire century.

In 1949 the exact location of the initial find was discovered, and the cave was given a thorough archaeological survey. More fragments of scrolls were uncovered, along with pieces of cloth, pottery and wood. Over the next seven years ten more caves containing ancient texts were found in the Qumran area, and the remains of around 850 different scrolls were discovered in total. The caves were named in the order that they were searched, and cave four, uncovered in 1952, proved the single biggest haul of artefacts with 15,000 fragments of 500

Part of a manuscript from the Dead Sea Scrolls.

different manuscripts. A complex of ancient structures close to the caves, referred to as the Qumran ruin, was also excavated.

What the scientists discovered was that the scrolls and the ruin both dated from between the third century BC and 68 AD, placing them around the time of Christ. It seems the texts formed the library of a Jewish sect, similar to the Essenes. The Essenes were a strict Torah-observing society, who disliked the established priesthood and may have actually been wiped-out by the Jerusalem based church. It is thought the ruins at Qumran formed part of their society, and the scrolls were hidden from the advancing Roman army around AD70. The truly fascinating thing about the scrolls is not so much their history, but what they actually say.

The scrolls have been deciphered and reconstructed by expert modern scholars. They tend to fall into two groups: texts concerned with religion and others revealing details of daily lives and history. There are copies of many biblical writings, and all but one book of the Old Testament. More interestingly, there are previously unseen psalms authored by King David and Joshua, and also some prophecies attributed to Ezekiel, Jeremiah and Daniel that do not appear in the Bible. The scrolls contain previously unknown stories about Enoch, Abraham and Noah. Similarly the lost words of Amram, Joseph, Judah, Levi and Naphtali are also revealed in the texts.

Surprisingly, given their date and proximity to New Testament events, the life of Jesus Christ is not mentioned. The scrolls are mainly written in Hebrew, but also feature passages in Aramaic and Greek. Some scrolls explain laws and codes of battle, whereas others recount poems and the philosophies of wise men. The most enigmatic information contained in the scrolls lists 64 places around Israel where ancient treasures are buried. It is suggested that not only gold and silver is hidden there, but many of the holy objects from the temple of Jerusalem were also deposited in distant, unknown places for safekeeping.

Although the scrolls were all discovered within eight years, the collection was scattered among universities, museums and scholarly institutions across the world. In 1954, some of the scrolls were even

Painstaking detective work on the Scrolls has allowed most of their contents to be read.

advertised for sale in the Wall Street Journal. Many of the scrolls were in terrible condition, so it became difficult to assemble a complete idea of what the texts revealed. During the 1960s and 70s much of the work that was done remained unpublished, so public interest in the scrolls waned. In the last decade however, there has been a renewed commitment to provide complete collections of photographs, translations and explanations to the wider world. This seems vitally important. Not only do the scrolls represent an amazing historical discovery, they also chronicle a time essentially interwoven with our understanding of the Biblical World.

Gef the Talking Mongoose

WHEN IS A GHOST not a ghost? When it is a talking mongoose! In 1931 the Irving family started hearing strange sounds coming from the attic and walls of their farm in Dalby on the Isle of Man. James Irving, his wife Margaret and their daughter Voirrey were sure a large animal was scampering around the house out of sight. The noises it made were so loud, plates fall and hanging pictures moved. Over time, it began making bizarre hissing and crying sounds. James Irving decided to make animal noises at it, and, to his astonishment, the creature started doing these impressions back at him.

He decided to teach the beast a few words, and within weeks the creature could speak perfectly. It said its name was Gef, and it was a mongoose born on 7th June 1852 in Delhi, India. Gef refused to appear in front of the Irvings, and was known to be quite rude. When the Irvings threatened to leave him, he calmed down. The family and the mongoose grew close, and he even let them stroke him through a hole in the wall.

Eventually, the story of Gef spread, although when reporters came from the mainland, many were unimpressed with the phenomenon. They believed it was actually Voirrey who was creating the voice. In 1937 the Irvings sold the farm and were believed to have taken Gef with them. However, in 1947, the new owner claimed to have shot a strange, mongoose-like animal outside the house.

The idea of a mongoose in the Isle of Man is not quite as bizarre as it first appears. In 1912 a local farmer did import a group of the animals to kill rabbits on his land. However, most present-day researchers believe if Gef was anything, then he was probably a poltergeist. But there is one last interesting fact; in India they have a strange old legend. They say that over time, and with the right teacher, the mongoose can learn to speak.

THE GREAT FLOOD

JESUS CHRIST HIMSELF referred to 'The Flood' but it is not only Christians who believe in the story. Jews believe in accounts of the disaster described in the Holy Torah whilst Muslims have references in the Koran. The first historical record of the disaster appeared in eighteenth century BC Babylonian writings, whilst the ancient Epic of Gilgamesh is also concerned with a great flood. 'Flood' traditions and references exist in 300 different cultures around the world; Ancient Greeks, Romans and Native Americans all have fables of a terrible flood that left only a few survivors. There are suggestions that the Noah flood may have been the same event that destroyed Atlantis. Although tradition and mythology has often represented strong circumstantial evidence, recent provable scientific knowledge has been crucial in helping to support the 'Great Flood' theory.

The scientific approach began in the 1990s

Noah's Ark: many cultures around the world tell stories of cataclysmic floods which swept away their predecessors.

Evidence from the bottom of the Black Sea proves it was once dry land. Was it drowned in Noah's flood?

when two geologists from Columbia University, William Ryan and Walter Pitman, pieced together clues that they believed suggested a great ancient flood actually did occur. Ryan and Pitman formulated a theory which proposed that the European ice sheets melted about 7,500 years ago as the world rapidly grew warmer following the last Ice Age. The excess water caused the Mediterranean to overflow into the Black Sea which Ryan and Pitman believe was initially a shallow, land-locked fresh water lake with river-fed fertile plains surrounding it. They suggest that it was a heavily populated area which was completely drowned by the rising sea levels.

Ryan and Pitman suggest that as the ice melted, the Black Sea rose by as much as six inches per day, with water rushing in at 200 times the rate of Niagara Falls. Within a year,

60,000 square miles of land was lost under water, and the fresh water basin became a salt-water extension of the ocean. The farmers and settlers who had relied on the natural environment of the area were forced away, not only by rising water levels, but also by the loss of their fresh water resources. Ryan and Pitman believe the ancient lake shoreline now lies around 5,000 feet below the present water level. Sediment core samples take from the centre of the Black Sea have provided fascinating evidence. Plant roots and mud cracks in these samples suggest a dry riverbed covered in a layer of mud, which indicates a great flood.

As a continuation of Ryan and Pitman's work, the underwater explorer Robert Ballard decided to study the area in 1999. Ballard was the man who discovered remains of the Titanic and, using highly technological equipment, he and his team found a previous coastline 550 feet deep and 20 miles out into the Black Sea. They took samples which included freshwater and saltwater molluscs from the ancient seabed. Apart from the well-preserved geographical and oceanographic features of the underwater area which pointed to a coastline flooding gradually, the freshwater molluscs species were carbon dated at an age older than the saltwater molluscs. Scientists also discovered that the fresh water molluscs all seemed to die at the same time, suggesting an immediate change in environment for them. The youngest freshwater shells were found to be 7,460 years old, whereas the oldest saltwater creatures dated from 6,820 years ago. This suggests the flood happened somewhere between those two dates, confirming Ryan and Pitman's original theory.

Ballard returned to the area in September 2000, and discovered some even more fascinating revelations. They found ancient tools and rubbish sites, and crucially, a prehistoric dwelling. The wooden-beamed man-made structure contained ceramic vessels and stone tools and was found 300 feet down. The team referred to it as 'Noah's House,' although radiocarbon dating has proved it was too young to be from Noah's time. However, it did provide real evidence that the area was inhabited before the 'Great Flood' and would have produced witnesses to the catastrophic event. The condition of the house also showed that the flood had happened at such a speed that surface waves had not had time to batter the building before consuming it.

These theories and discoveries offer many fascinating avenues for further study. Anthropologists are interested to see how population movements are caused by terrible disasters and how ancient races have passed on their great tales using only word of mouth. Geologists and oceanographers are fascinated by immense sea-level changes and flood lands, particularly with the looming threat of global warming. For scholars, historians and the religious alike, the confirmation of an amazing Biblical story is a welcome change in an age of legend-destroying scientific discovery.

HINDU STATUES DRINKING MILK

O**N 21ST SEPTEMBER 1995**, reports started to come out of New Delhi of Hindu statues drinking milk. Worshippers were offering spoonfuls of the substance as a sacred gift, and the symbolic carvings of Lord Shiva and Ganesha were actually consuming it. Queues built up around temples, and the local authorities had to increase the city's milk supply by 100,000 litres because of a shortage. Sceptics immediately suggested it was a case of mass hallucination, or that the porous quality of the statues that created the

Statue of a Hindu goddess, not drinking milk.

Right: Saint Bernadette of Lourdes. The town has become the destination for hundreds of thousands of Catholic pilgrims a year.

phenomenon. Others said the milk was just being spilt, but the ground around the statues did not hold anywhere near the amount of milk that was being offered.

Certainly, those who came had no doubts that it was a true miracle, and as Indian communities heard about the phenomenon, other reports about similar events appeared across the world. By the next day, Hindu worshipers were standing in long lines outside London temples, eager to offer the statues milk. Anila Premji was one lady who waited during the night to attend the Vishwa temple in Southall, west London, to offer a spoonful to a marble figure of Nandi, a bull ridden by Shiva. 'I held the spoon out level, and the milk just disappeared,' she said. At the main Swaminarayan temple in London, the situation was so busy that authorities were refusing entry to people bringing their own milk cartons.

In Canada, Germany and the United States the miracles were continued. Hindu worshipers at Chatsworth Hindu Temple in California also reported milk being accepted by their idols. Stories were run by Reuters, CNN, the BBC and most of the world's major newspapers. Despite sceptics giving scientific explanations, the devoutly religious said it was a sign of God. Even those Hindu worshippers who did not regularly attend the temples witnessed the events and said they felt a reassured sense of an almighty power protecting them. Perhaps that is the point. No matter what practical explanations are advanced, sometimes a resurgent faith in a divine presence is a great comfort for those who want to believe.

LOURDES

ON 7TH JANUARY 1844 Marie Bernarde Soubirous was born. She was the first child of Francois Soubirous, a poor miller from Lourdes in Southern France, and his wife Louise. She was a fragile child, and such was her small stature she acquired the name Bernadette. Her father's lack of money meant she was often sent away to be cared for by relatives and friends, and in the summer of 1857 she went to stay with Marie Aravant in the nearby town of Batres. Aravant enjoyed having the girl at her home, but was concerned about her religious development. She tried to teach Bernadette about the Bible, but repeatedly grew impatient as the teenager failed to show any aptitude for the subject. Finally, Marie Aravant asked a local priest for his advice.

He said Bernadette should be sent back to Lourdes for Catechism classes.

And so, shortly after her 14th birthday, the girl arrived back in her hometown. On 11th February 1858, Bernadette was with two friends collecting wood from the shore of the river Gave, to the west of Lourdes. She decided to walk to a great stone promontory known as the 'Big Rock' or Massabieille, which was a deserted spot next to the river. At the base of the cliff there was a 25-foot deep and 40-foot wide natural hollow. Bernadette heard a noise and looked up. The events that followed would change Bernadette and this area of France forever.

As Bernadette raised her head, she saw a vision of a beautiful lady dressed in white and praying the Rosary. The apparition disappeared but Bernadette returned to the grotto and saw her again. On her third appearance, on 18th February, the lady spoke and asked the girl to come to their area each day for two weeks. Bernadette did as she was told. One day, the lady told Bernadette to wash herself in the grotto's spring water. There was no spring in the area, so the girl dug into the mud and bathed in its damp earthiness. By the next day, a strong spring of fresh water had manifested. On the 13th encounter with the vision, the lady asked for a chapel to be built in her honour, and on the 16th appearance the woman revealed her identity as the 'Immaculate Conception.' In total, Bernadette had seen the Holy Virgin Mother 18 times, with the last vision occurring on 16th July 1858.

Very quickly, many of those who drank or bathed in the grotto's spring were reporting miraculous cures. By 28th July 1858 the Bishop of Tarbes had instigated an investigative commission. For over three and a half years this group of eminent clergymen, doctors and scientist studied the claims made by Bernadette and worshipers at the

281. LOURDES - Intérieur des Piscines.

Inside the spring at Lourdes.

grotto. On 18th January 1862 they ruled that Bernadette herself was an entirely normal girl who really had seen the Virgin Mary. The cures attributed to the spring at Massabieille were declared real, but inexplicable, and the authorities agreed to build a chapel in homage to the Holy Mother there, thus providing the focal point for pilgrims.

The main Basilica at Lourdes now comprises three chapels and there are other churches nearby. The largest one in the area, the Basilica of St Pius X, can hold 30,000 people, which is particularly useful as the site is visited by about a million pilgrims each year. Many travel there simply to show their respect, or to receive religious solace. Others who go are critically unwell and hope the healing waters will restore their mortal spirit. In total, there have been nearly 4,000 recoveries from illnesses, which have ranged from tuberculosis, sores and blindness to deafness and cancers. There have also been 65 miracles certified by the Catholic Church attributed to Our Lady of Lourdes.

Bernadette herself was not so lucky. In 1866 she joined the sisters of Nevers at the convent of Saint Gildard. Always frail, she continued to suffer from various illnesses and died on 16th April 1879 at the age of 35. In 1925, Bernadette's perfectly preserved remains were transferred from the convent chapel to a glass casket in the Nevers chapel. It appeared that her body had survived better in death than it had in life and a Doctor Talon, who helped exhume her, later wrote an article for a medical journal saying the state of preservation was not a 'natural phenomenon.' Bernadette was canonised in 1935, and is now the subject of pilgrimage in her own right.

MODERN MIRACLES

ALL OF THE RELIGIOUS mysteries in this section have some relationship, in one way or another, to miracles. They are inexplicable, God inspired phenomena. Sceptics argue that the human condition is such that we naturally want to believe in miracles, and the phenomenon has such an attraction that even atheists and pragmatists are sometimes overcome by these bizarre events. For as long as Man can remember, different religions and races have understood that some occurrences are instigated by a deity and beyond our comprehension. In recent years the abundance of phenomena has increased dramatically. Some say it is due to a resurgence in spirituality teamed with a truly worldwide, 24 hour media. Others believe it has had more to do with an encroaching millennium fever which induced expectations of a great happening as we crossed into the 21st century. For whatever reason, some of the modern reports of miracles have been truly amazing.

One of first miracles to be captured by the world's media occurred in April 1968. In the town of Zeitun in Egypt apparitions of the Virgin Mary started to mysteriously appear. These bizarre sights lasted for over three years and were viewed by over a million people firsthand. Countless more across the globe saw them after they were filmed by the Egyptian television and photographed by the world's press. Even Egypt's Marxist dictator, President Nasser, who was an atheist by nature, visited the site and saw the apparitions in person. To check the phenomenon was not a hoax or a prank, Egyptian police scoured a 95 mile radius around Zeitun. They searched for any suspicious equipment that may have been the source of the display, but found nothing.

This type of phenomenon, the spontaneous apparition, has become one of the most widespread modern miracles. In December 1995 an image of Christ's face was imprinted in a granite rock in Australia. Julian Webb, the wheat farmer on whose land the rock is found, said that one night he saw a beam of light focus on the solid stone slab. As he watched the illuminated granite, the face of Jesus slowly formed on the rock and remained there. Webb does not consider himself a religious man, nor is he a regular church-goer, but is convinced he witnessed a miracle. On Christmas Day that same year, people all around the city of Teheran in Iran reported seeing the image of Christ appear on fences and building walls. Despite the fact the overwhelming majority of the population are Muslim, all the witnesses believed they had seen visions of Jesus.

These apparitions at the end of 1995 were merely an opening chapter to a huge range of visions reported around the globe the following year. An image of the Virgin Mary appeared on a roof of a San Francisco church, and visitors reported smelling an unsourced scent of rose petals. Another church in South Australia had a picture of the Holy Mother manifest itself on an inside wall and a spring of water with healing properties was found underneath the building. The most impressive example occurred for three weeks around Christmas 1996, when almost half a million people saw the Virgin Mary on a black glass building in Florida. The image measured 50 feet wide and 35 feet tall, and remained inexplicable despite the fact that local scientists and academics studied the apparition at length.

It is not only established church-based religions that have been caught up in this recent tide of miracles – Native Americans have also been experiencing their own unusual holy events. To these people, the birth of white buffalo is a truly miraculous occurrence akin to some of the greatest Christian miracles. Three different years in the last decade, 1993, 1994 and 1996, all saw the arrival of pale buffalo calves. Add to this the bizarre visions appearing before respected tribal leaders across the United States, and indigenous Americans were convinced of an end-of-millennium religious spectacle.

To a great extent, the importance of a miracle is dependent on a person's reaction to it. Scientists and sceptics feel that truth and practical explanation is the only important factor. However, can there be any real crime in an event not instigated by human means which offers confirmation of beliefs and helps people to live peaceful lives?

NOAH'S ARK

THE BIBLE SAYS that God warned Noah that he was planning to wipe out Mankind because his sins had grown too much. He told Noah that he wanted to save two of each kind of animal, and Noah and his family, so that Creation could continue after the Great Flood. Noah was instructed to build a large wooden Ark 45 feet long, 75 feet wide and 45 feet high, which could house and protect them as the waters raged. For 40 days and 40 nights the rain poured and the sea rose until the Earth was completely covered. Both the Bible and the Koran say that the Ark came to rest on Mount Ararat as the water subsided, and that is where the focus of most Ark-hunters attempts has been.

The mountain lies in the far east corner of Turkey close to borders with Russia, Iran and Iraq. The highest peak is just under 17,000 ft high, but the Ark itself is believed to lie a little further down, in a chasm called the Ahora Gorge. In the gorge there is an ice-covered mountain called Al Judi, which is where the Koran places the beached vessel. However, this area is not easy to explore, and is only accessible for a couple of months each year. Melting ice and rock falls make the Ahora Gorge particularly treacherous, and rolling mists, hidden glaciers and altitude difficulties have ended the research of many adventurers. Historically it has always been a politically unstable region, close to many of the world's violent hotspots and the Turkish government has frequently discouraged any organised investigations. The locals themselves are also less than helpful, and one possible resting-place of the ark is said to be guarded by fierce indigenous tribesmen.

Despite this, countless researchers searching for the Ark have ventured into the area, and may have discovered proof of a wooden construction locked in the ice caps. The most common find has been machined and treated timbers, uncovered in areas completely devoid of natural woodland. In 1876 a British ambassador to Turkey found such remains when climbing Mount Ararat. The timber he discovered had been hand-hewn and fixed with an extremely hard black covering. Almost 80 years later, in 1955, an explorer called Fernand Navarra and his son Rafael discovered some wooden beams in a crevice on the mountain. They took samples of the wood and these have been carbon dated as being around 4000 years old.

Sightings of the Ark itself have also been documented. The first modern encounter is said to have happened in 1856 what a group of young English atheist scientists climbed the mountain with two local guides. Despite everyone swearing to keep the discovery secret, two members of the search team independently revealed details on their deathbeds. In the 1910's, an official Russian military expedition commissioned by the Czar, claimed to have found Noah's Ark and took measurements and photographs of the vessel. The results and reports sent back to the Czar were all lost or destroyed during the Communist Revolution, but many independent witnesses account for the events that occurred. Crucially, everybody who claims to have found the remains has done so in the same area of Mount Ararat.

In more recent years, aerial technology has provided an overall picture of the mountain,

The animals go in two by two. Has the final resting place of Noah's Ark been finally uncovered?

but has suggested the Ark may lie somewhere different. In 1949 a US Air Force mission photographed an unusual feature 15,500 feet up on the northwestern plateau of Mount Ararat on the other side from the Ahora Gorge. The images appear to show the bow of a ship poking out of a glacier. The phenomenon given the name the 'Ararat Anomaly' and resurfaced in the 1970s when secret military satellites were able to focus on the area from space. Since then, more high-powered, clearer and commercial satellites have allowed researchers a better chance of examining the strange structure. It seems to be 600 feet long and some experts

believe it may be the wooden ribbed structure of an ancient boat.

Other Ark investigators believe it could be simply an old rock formation, an old fortress, or even a crashed aeroplane. Of course, the only way researchers can gather definite evidence is to be near the site on the ground. But increased tension between Turkey and the area's Kurdish population has hampered exploration attempts, and the recent instability in nearby Iraq has also added to the region's pressures. Until a team of archaeological experts can examine the photographed remains firsthand, the mystery of Noah's Ark will never be solved.

SAINT-MÉDARD

WHEN THE DEACON of Paris, François de Paris, died in May 1727, great swathes of mourners attended his funeral. The congregation was sorrowful, for François was only 37, and was said to have holy healing powers. The emotional crowd followed his coffin as it was placed behind the high altar in the small church of Saint-Médard. One by one, the congregation slowly trundled past the body, paying their respects and laying tokens of affection. One crippled boy shuffled up to the coffin with the help of his father. As they looked onto the clergyman's peaceful face, the boy was suddenly hit by a powerful physical reaction. Members of the crowd struggled to control his squirming body as it was hit by a series of savage convulsions. They pulled him away from the altar and the convulsions stopped. The boy opened his eyes, stood up, and with a look of complete joyous realisation, began dancing and singing around the church, his malformed right leg now taking the weight as easily as his left.

This event was the beginning of an extensive range of miracles that happened over a five-year period and originated at the churchyard of Saint-Médard. What is most remarkable about this series of unexplained incidents is the complete integrity and intelligence of those that witnessed the events. Although many of the Deacon's followers were poor, unhealthy and perhaps easily fooled, others who observed these bizarre happenings were lawyers, scientists and respected public figures. The most detailed and believable witness accounts came from a magistrate, Louis-Basile Carré de Montgéron. Montgéron had a lawyer friend by the name of Louis Adrien de Paige who had long described the Saint-Médard events, but Montgéron was convinced his friend was being fooled. Despite not particularly wishing to go to the churchyard, Montgéron relented and agreed to visit.

The two men arrived at Saint-Médard on the morning of 7th September 1731. What Montgéron saw immediately shocked him; women writhing on the floor; men beating other women with wooden and metal bars; there was even one woman whose nipples were being twisted in a metal clamp. All the time, the women did not seem to feel pain, in fact they pleaded for more punishment. Paige explained that this treatment cured the women of their deformities and diseases. Things quickly became more disturbing for Montgéron when he saw a teenage girl sitting at a table eating from a plate. As Montgéron approached, he could see that the girl was eating human faeces and drinking human urine. The girl had previously suffered from a psychological problem that caused her to constantly wash her hands. Not only was she cured of this neurosis, but the most amazing part of the episode occurred as she appeared to begin vomiting. Out of her mouth poured pure cow's milk.

As Montgéron stumbled around the churchyard, he came upon a group of women who were cleaning infected cuts and boils by licking the poisons from them. Montgéron watched as a young child, suffering form the most appallingly diseased leg had her bandages removed. Even the woman who was to perform the cleansing needed to pray for strength. But after a moment she began, removing and swallowing the festering tissue, leaving a perfectly clean leg. During this first visit Montgéron saw enough miracles to leave him emotionally exhausted. He continued to revisit the churchyard many times, collecting enough evidence for an incredible book. That year, he was thrown into prison for handing a copy of the tome to a disgusted King Louis XV. But Montgéron would not be silenced, and published three further books demonstrating an honest, serious examination of the miracles in the churchyard of Saint-Médard.

The French authorities grew concerned that these miracles would undermine their power and the king tried to close the churchyard. At the time, the writer Voltaire quipped that 'God is forbidden by order of the King to perform any more miracles in the cemetery of Saint-Médard.' When soldiers were sent to seize the church land they failed totally. The stories of Saint-Médard spread and persisted for years, and the Scottish philosopher, David Hume wrote that there was never 'so great a number of miracles ascribed to one person,' as those attributed to François de Paris. It is a truly enduring mystery.

STIGMATA

STIGMATA HAVE BEEN such well-documented, historical phenomena that many sceptics have been forced to accept their legitimacy. The affliction creates marks on the hands, feet, side and brow which reflect the wounds Christ suffered on the cross. The marks often bleed or secrete a liquid, and can appear and disappear in a matter of hours. It is usually only saints and the most devoutly religious who experience stigmata. It not only leaves a physical representation of Christ's wounds, but stigmatics often feel pain near the marks, and many report a lifelong sense of despair and suffering. Some even feel the lashing of whips across their backs. Religious followers believe that the pain is an integral part of stigmata.

The first celebrated stigmatic was Saint Francis of Assisi. His holy marks appeared in 1222 and were of an extent never

subsequently equalled. The skin on his hands and feet actually grew out of the wounds to form calluses in the shape of nails. Since his time, there have been over three hundred reported stigmatics, sixty-two of which were saints. Georgio Bongiavani is one of the most well known recent sufferers of stigmata. In his case, wounds on his hands and forehead seem to appear and disappear almost at will. The explanation for stigmata is still a mystery. Doctors have recorded that blood secreted by the wounds is a different type to the stigmatic's blood group or is an unknown liquid, or even exudes a perfume.

A popular theory is that stigmata are psychosomatic afflictions brought on by extreme levels of worship. Some believe stigmatics unconsciously bring about these wounds by their devotion to Christ. Many stigmatics have reported their wounds appearing in their greatest intensity around the holy days of Easter, when sufferers are most engrossed by religious events. Similarly, each stigmatic's wounds generally correspond to the marks on the statue of the person they most often worship. If the statue is nailed through the wrist and ankles, their wounds appear in the wrist and ankles. But of course, there is another theory; that stigmata are sent by God as a gift to only the most holy.

TURIN SHROUD

THE TURIN SHROUD is probably the most famous religious relic in the world. The cloth measures thirteen-and-a-half feet long by four-and-a-half feet wide, and clearly depicts the body of a bearded man, said to be Jesus Christ. Its legend states that it was used by Joseph of Arimathea to wrap the body of Christ after his crucifixion. Its first appearance in recorded history came in 1357, in the little village of Lirey in France. It was then taken to Chambéry, in the Savoy region of the country in 1457, and it was there in 1532 that the shroud was almost destroyed in a fierce fire. This experience left charred marks on the corner of the folds in the fabric, and in 1578 it was taken to Turin where it has remained ever since. The Catholic Church is convinced that the shroud genuinely possesses an amazing physical record of Christ's body, and the cloth is now only shown to the public on rare occasions.

However, organised religion has not always been so accepting. Research has uncovered documents from 1389 written by the Bishop of Troyes and Pope Clement VII. Lirey was in the Bishop's diocese, and he asked the Pontiff to publicly rule that the shroud was merely a painting. He stated that the image had actually been painted by an artist, originally as decoration, but the priests in Lirey had started duping the local public into believing it was Christ's authentic death shroud. The Pope's conclusion bowed to the Bishop's wishes, but was hardly resolute. He declared that the shroud could keep being exhibited, but each time it was shown, the local priest had to announce to the assembled public that the relic only depicted a painted copy of Christ's real cloth.

Over the years such practices fell away, and authenticity of the shroud was assumed. The early days of the enlightened age of science seemed to corroborate this belief. In 1898 photographic experts revealed the image was actually a negative picture, and seen in reverse tones, the outline showed a much more detailed view of the body. By 1901, Dr Paul Vignon produced a theory that such a phenomenon was caused by ammonia emanating from Christ's dead body after his terrible death. Vignon believed the resulting image was therefore beyond the ability of any forger, and must have been authentic.

But that is not the view of more modern appraisals, and in 1979 Dr Walter McCrone conducted a series of advanced scientific tests on samples of the shroud. Using microscopic and microchemical forensic techniques, McCrone and his associates discovered particles of red ochre and vermilion pigment mixed with a tempera medium. No blood was found on the cloth. Tempera was a substance widely used by medieval painters, and recent theories suggest that the original light yellow paint has turned dark brown over the centuries. Similarly, the background cloth has actually faded to a paler hue, thus causing the strange negative image effect, misunderstood by earlier researchers.

The most famous and conclusive recent tests involved radiocarbon dating of the shroud. In 1988, laboratories in America, Switzerland and England performed examinations on sections of the cloth. All three concluded the material was produced between 1260 and 1390 AD, thereby fitting

The Turin Shroud: the face of Jesus, or 14th century fake?

in with the historical recorded period of the picture's production. There is also common sense evidence against the shroud's authenticity. Firstly, the Greek New Testament itself claims Christ was actually wrapped in strips of linen, not a whole sheet. We also have no idea of the provenance of the shroud before the fourteenth century. Finally, the image on the shroud has quite obviously faded and damaged over the last few centuries, whilst it has been in the care of the Catholic Church, although when it was first viewed, witnesses stated that the picture was bright and vibrant.

Despite these questions surrounding the shroud, some investigators continue to search for proof of its authenticity. One recent theory states the samples taken for carbon dating were contaminated by fungi and bacteria that had grown in the cloth over the centuries. This idea is also used as an explanation for some dressings on Egyptian mummies that have been carbon dated at an age many hundreds of years later than the remains they cover. But most of the scientific community is convinced that by combining and corroborating the evidence, the Turin Shroud is simply a medieval painting that subsequently assumed mystical beliefs. Even so, it can be confidently claimed that the shroud is the world's greatest explained mystery.

VEIL OF VERONICA

THE TURIN SHROUD is not the only ancient artefact purporting to show a mysterious imprint of Christ's features. Christian legend tells of a fabled, linen veil which also inexplicably shows the face of Jesus. It is a cloth said to have miraculous healing powers and supernatural qualities. Just like the Turin Shroud, it is also the source of controversy. However, the veil has more intriguing mysteries surrounding it than just what caused the image. The Vatican claims it has been holding the cloth in its archive continuously since the twelfth century, but in 1999 an expert in Christian art history, who works for Vatican organisations, said he had found the real veil hidden in a remote Italian abbey. So what exactly is the world supposed to believe?

When Christ was carrying his cross through Jerusalem on the way to being crucified at Cavalry, a woman stepped forward and used her veil to wipe the sweat and blood from His face. As a sign if gratitude, He left an image of his likeness stained on the cloth. Although this episode is not mentioned in the scriptures, legend says the woman's name was Veronica. She is said to have kept the cloth and realised that it had holy healing powers. She took the veil to Rome where she used it to cure Emperor Tiberius of a malady, and then left it in the care of Pope Clement and the Catholic Church.

Historical records show that the veil was in Rome from at least the fourth century. In 1297 it was placed in the Vatican Basilica and was the subject of worship from pilgrims who believed the picture was indeed the genuine likeness of Christ. The image itself was almost identical to the face seen on the Turin Shroud. In 1608 the area of the Basilica displaying the veil was demolished in order to be redesigned, and the cloth was placed in the Vatican's archives. Under tight security, it was brought out once a year for public viewing. Or so Catholics believed.

On 3rd June 1999, a professor of Christian art history at the Vatican's Gregorian University, and official advisor to the Papal Commission for the Cultural History of the Church, revealed he had successfully completed a 13-year investigation to find the real Veil of Veronica. A German Jesuit, Heinrich Pfeiffer explained that the artefact annually displayed was merely a copy that the Vatican had created so as not to disappoint pilgrims.

He claimed to have actually found the true relic in an abbey in the tiny village of Monopello, high in the Italian Apennine mountains. Records in the village's monastery revealed that the wife of a jailed soldier stole the veil in 1608, and sold it to a Monopellan nobleman to release her husband from prison. The nobleman gave it to the abbey's Capuchin monks, who have kept it in the monastery and revered it as a sacred icon ever since.

The veil Pfeiffer found is an almost transparent cloth 6.7 inches wide and 9.4 inches long. The dark red image on it depicts a bearded man with long hair and open eyes.

The Veil of Veronica on display in the Vatican.

There are also red drop marks, which are believed to be blood. The picture itself seems to appear and disappear in different light – a quality that Pfeiffer says would have been viewed as supernatural in less advanced times. Pfeiffer also revealed that ultraviolet testing confirmed that veil the image was not created by paint, and the image has been infused identically on both sides.

Sceptics are not convinced. They believe the extremely thin nature of the cloth allowed the image to seep through to be the same on each side. Many believe the similarities between the veil and the Turin Shroud occur because the veil was a deliberate copy of the larger cloth. They also point out the fact that Veronica's meeting with Christ has never been historically documented, and her name itself is a work of fiction – being an amalgamation of the Latin words for 'true image,' or 'vera-icon.'

The only scientific way of determining the age of the cloth is by carbon dating, but its brittle, delicate state means it could be irreparably damaged during any such tests. For Pfeiffer there is no doubt about the religious authenticity of the veil, and he is entirely convinced that his find is the true artefact. But for other Catholics, it is not so easy. Even if they accept the legend, which veil do they chose as the genuine relic?

WEEPING STATUES

THE PHENOMENON OF weeping or crying religious statues is one of the oldest and most stereotypical images of holy powers in Catholicism. Ireland, South America and southern Europe all have well documented accounts of Virgin Mary figurines seeping strange liquids. And, whilst sceptics believe there are good reasons to doubt the validity of such occurrences, to the local populations they are often only explainable under the term 'miracle.'

In November 1992, a six-inch-high, blue and white porcelain statue of the Virgin Mary began weeping blood in Santiago, Chile. The figurine, which belonged to a local housewife, became an attraction for local people in the La Cisterna district and was even tested by Chilean police. Doctors at the Santiago coroner's office discovered that the liquid produced at the statue's eyes was type O-4 human blood.

A similar event happened in the small village of Mura, 35 miles north of Barcelona in Spain. Outside the village church a two-foot-high marble statue of the Virgin Mary had been set on a seven-foot-high pedestal. In March 1998, the local priest, Luis Costa, discovered it was crying tears of blood. Mura residents were convinced the phenomenon was genuine. The statue had not been tampered with, and further investigation revealed the blood was emanating from the figure in a particularly human way.

Sceptics are quick to dismiss such stories. Some promote fanciful theories that water is soaked up by the base of the statues, mixes with red clay inside them, and then appears through the head as blood. Others are convinced these instances have been created through the use of a simple magic trick. Certainly, it is true that the actual point when blood appears on such statues is rarely witnessed. By diverting people's attention, it is easy to interfere with the figurines unnoticed. But these explanations fail to alter the effect on a credulous public. Although it is important to discover the truth, this type of religious mysticism is a pleasant way to remind us that there are still some things in life that we just can't explain.

A pious believer attempts to be healed by a statue.

PSYCHIC POWERS AND PHENOMENA

Auras and Kirlian Photography

Just as every living creation gives out heat, gasses and energy, so it is believed they emit an aura of vitality, that is to say, a glow of colour around the body which reveals its health, mood and thoughts. The idea of auras is a concept that has been around from the beginning of time. Even though most of us cannot detect them, there are psychic people who can see these indications of life force. The challenge in recent years has been to find a way of recording auras so ordinary people can view them. Aura enthusiasts believe we will be able to use them to help solve health, psychological and emotional problems, and perhaps even understand other mystical remedies.

Our knowledge of auras comes solely from the psychics who can see them. They say that the colour of an individual's aura, and the distance it radiates from a body, often provides vital information about the general wellbeing of the person. The hue and intensity of the aura are said to fluctuate constantly as individuals change moods, thoughts and levels of fatigue. As study in the area has increased, so too has a widely agreed catalogue of aura qualities and an understanding of what they mean. For example, a green aura reflects intellectual factors, whilst any brown or grey shades reflect disease. However, science has not gathered any definitive results, and different techniques in photography are constantly being evolved to try to capture auras on a solid substance.

The first person to use auras for medical purposes was Walter Kilner, the head of the electro-therapy department at St Thomas' Hospital in London in 1911. Kilner discovered that just by looking through coloured glass he could see an outline of light shrouding the patient's body. He noticed that the light changed shape, intensity and colour as the patient's health altered. Kilner was the only one who could see the light, and it was not until 1939 that his discoveries were taken any further. Semyon Kirlian, a Russian hospital electrician, stumbled by chance upon a completely unique method of photography. He realised that by placing a living object on a photographic plate and running a high voltage through it, the most amazing image of strange colours appeared as a halo around the subject.

Kirlian and his wife, Valentina, perfected the technique. The first photograph they took showed a leaf with millions of orange and turquoise light dots seemingly emanating from the leaf's veins, and a bizarre aura around the leaf edges. Over time they conducted many experiments and even developed an instrument that would show auras in motion. They noted that whilst healthy, vital subjects created pictures with the most distinct, radiant outlines – withered and dying subjects would result in very weak auras.

Kirlian also proposed and demonstrated the theory that different colours emanated with different moods, feelings and thoughts. A most fascinating experiment took place when a visiting scientist gave them two apparently identical leaves to study. The Kirlians were puzzled because one seemed to have a very strange aura, and yet it appeared normal.

In the 1970s and 80s Thelma Moss, a para-psychologist at the University of California, became convinced in the power of auras for medical purposes. She promoted the view that Kirlian's discovery was a way of showing 'bioenergy' as a tangible, provable subject, and even visited the Soviet Union to discuss techniques with paranormal researchers there. She wanted to use Kirlian auras as a diagnostic tool, and believed the subject represented the next major step forward for the medical establishment. Unfortunately, Moss died in 1997 without fully realising her aim.

In fact, Kirlian photography is seen by the established scientific community as being a very unreliable way of determining illnesses. It has been pointed out that moisture, air pressure and voltage all have a marked effect on the resulting picture. However, aura enthusiasts are convinced we all have a demonstrable life force atmosphere surrounding us. They say that it is only a matter of time before some unquestionable technique is devised, and a whole new world of personal care is unveiled.

DOWSING

THE OLD GAG where a man with a forked stick is searching for water is very well known. Initially he finds nothing, but as he approaches a tree, some strong power starts pulling the end of the stick downwards. The man looks triumphant, his talent and techniques vindicated. He then spots a rather self-satisfied dog standing next to the tree with a leg cocked in the air! The process the man used is called dowsing, and it can be used to find oil, gold, water, and even golf balls. It is known as one of the oldest of psychic powers, and connects man directly with the earth, but does dowsing really work?

Over the centuries, dowsers have made many appearances in mankind's traditions. It is said that cave drawings in Spain and Iraq show dowsers working in prehistoric times, and woodcuts from ancient China and Britain support the long heritage of dowsing. During the Middle Ages, dowsers were vilified as witches or devil worshippers; Martin Luther even claimed that dowsing was 'the work of the devil.' However, history also shows that many official groups have placed their trust in dowsers. German dowsers were apparently invited to assist British miners during the reign of Queen Elizabeth I, and it is claimed that modern military organisations actively employ them. General Patten was said to have used dowsers to find water to replace the wells destroyed by German forces during the Second World War, Similarly, the US Marine Corps apparently used dowsers to find mines

Dowsing for water: are water dowsers on to something real, or just wasting their time?

laid during the Vietnam War, and the British Army followed suit in the Falklands War.

The most common method dowsers employ is to walk around the area in which they are searching whilst holding their dowsing tools. These can be forked branches which point down when the dowser is above the thing searched for, or, more commonly, are two L-shaped rods made of copper, wood or wire held in each hand. The rods sit in the palms of the dowser with the longest side of the 'L' pointing forwards. When the dowser approaches the hunted substance, the rods swivel in the palm to touch each other, forming a cross. Another way of dowsing is to use a piece of string with a crystal on the end. The pendulum gently swings and the dowser is subtly guided to what they are looking for. The most impressive display is when dowsers are not even in the area to be searched, and simply use their dowsing technique over a map to locate an object or substance.

There are a number of theories as to why the rods move. Some believe it is electromagnetic power or other earth forces. However, the most likely explanation is involuntary nerve signals sent to the dowser's palms. It is generally accepted that dowsing is not controlled by physical or chemical influences, but more by the psychic ability of the dowser. It is suggested that, over time and with practise, the dowser can improve their talents and success rate. There have been some quite striking results from experienced dowsers. In a 1995 report by Hans-Dieter Betz, a physicist at the University of Munich, it was claimed that some dowsers achieved a 96% success rate in 691 drilling attempts to find water in Sri Lanka. The German government has since sponsored 100 dowsers to find water in arid areas of southern India.

The conventional scientific view is, however, that dowsing achieves no better results than pure guesswork. Indeed, there are a handful of high-profile competitions involving big money prizes for dowsers. One such challenge promises a million dollars if an 80% success rate in finding water flowing through underground pipes during controlled conditions can be achieved. The money has never been won.

Some dowsers do still use their skills to earn a healthy living – a select few act as advisors to mining and drilling companies searching for minerals. However, the fact is that scientists are always sceptical about phenomena that they cannot explain. But the great thing about dowsing is, unlike other psychic powers, it is an activity anybody can at least try. Who knows, if you practise hard enough, there is a million-dollar cheque just waiting to be cashed!

ESP AND PSYCHOKINESIS

EXTRA-SENSORY PERCEPTION (ESP) and Psychokinesis (PK) are the two powers that govern all self-controlled human mysteries. ESP is the ability to feel or understand events which are not apparent to the standard five senses, whereas psychokinesis is a natural force which can be used to physically affect the world, without there being any physical contact. Together, these two talents are known as psychic powers or psi, and many researchers believe they are inherent in us all. Other scientists think they are nothing but bunkum, hoaxes or magic tricks which have never been proven in controlled laboratory conditions.

The subject of ESP has been around for centuries under the guise of telepathy and clairvoyance, and there is some substance behind the possibility of its existence. Animals are known to have instincts and senses that are inexplicable if we rely purely on the five established receptors. For example, trained dogs can feel when an epileptic person will have a fit, and can give the sufferer enough of a warning for medication and safety precautions to be taken. Advocates of human ESP suggest we have similar powers ingrained with natural instincts, but our modern, comfortable lifestyles have allowed them to become dormant and unused.

The first scientifically tested experiments to investigate the subject of ESP were conducted by Joseph Banks Rhine in the 1930s. Rhine was a scientist at Duke University in Durham, USA, and developed the now archetypal ESP-testing, card guessing game. Rhine would ask the subjects in his experiments which one of five cards he was holding – it would either show a circle, a square, a plus sign, a star or three wavy lines. The pack would contain 25 cards, and the success rate of the subject compared to the pure statistics of probability gave a reading of whether some external, unknown sense was at play.

Rhine concluded that ESP was a genuine phenomenon that could be effected by the human involved in the experiment. He discovered that if people were relaxed and comfortable, their success rate would improve but if those being tested were bored, scared or simply disliked the notion of ESP, their results would actually be worse than probability. Character and situation are said to have great bearing on individual ESP sensitivity. Particularly stressful or traumatic scenarios are believed to encourage much more receptivity to instinctive senses. Those who call themselves psychics are said to be naturally in tune with their inherent powers, and can feel unexplained sensations as easily as normal people receive the known five.

These psychics are often the brunt of scientists' most fierce scepticism. Many researchers, who utterly disbelieve the notion of psi, point to the long history of so-called psychics being revealed as charlatans, con men or illusionists. Similarly they question every aspect of the controlled experiments used to prove the existence of ESP and point to the fact that successful tests are often unrepeatable. Some scientists are eager to state that there is no known force or sense that can be received or manipulated by the brain. If there are such things as brainwaves, then why can we not build a machine to receive them? It must also be highlighted that ESP tests can be proven successful just by pure luck playing a part, whereas psychokinesis experiments are far less susceptible to chance. Either people involved in psychokinesis experiments can make things move psychically or not, and any positive result would be a sensation.

Needless to say, the lack of public understanding of psychokinetic energy is due to the very fact there have not been any substantially successful tests, and that the proof we do have of its existence comes purely from anecdotal evidence. That said, the phenomenon of poltergeists is well documented – if not laboratory tested – and is believed to contain a great deal of psychokinetic influence.

Certainly, many traditional biologists and physicists would refute the existence of any forces that are not explained by known science and when such powers are reinforced by dubious evidence, their credibility is questioned further. However, the public perception of psi ability is quite different, and recent surveys have shown that two-thirds of American adults believe they have experienced some occurrence of ESP. In many ways, the subject is akin to the question of God, or the human soul. Are there actually forces we can feel and control, but which our intelligence cannot yet understand?

LEVITATION

MANY OF THOSE who have been known to levitate have had fervent and passionate states of mind. The early Christian Church believed levitation was a sign of demonic possession, and certainly it has been known to afflict the possessed. However, throughout the centuries, many holy people have also been able to lift themselves off the ground. The most famous was probably St Joseph of Copertino, born in 1603 in Apulia, Italy, who reached a state of religious ecstasy that allowed him to defy gravity. He is said to have levitated over a hundred times in his life, and it was the demonstration of his rapture-induced ability in front of Pope Urban VIII that led to his canonisation.

Eastern philosophies and religions teach that levitation can be achieved through a devoted study to fully harness the body's life force. This natural energy is called 'Ch'i' or 'Ki,' and is said to be controlled by extensive yogic training. The phenomenon of 'yogic hops,' where a person can make short levitational movements using transcendental meditation is also advanced by Eastern teachings. The focus is placed less on extreme emotion, but more on visualisation and breath control to summon up all latent energy within the body.

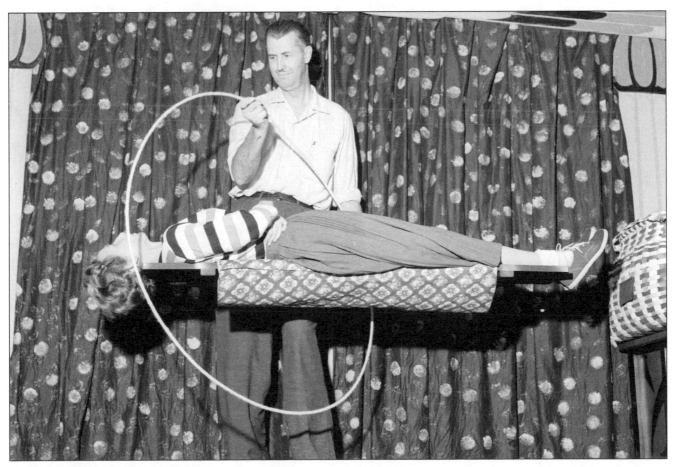

A visual illusion, but does levitation actually work?

Illusionist or the real thing? Opinion is sharply divided on the subject.

Some psychics also believe the power needed to levitate ourselves is a naturally inherent psychokinetic power. The nineteenth century medium Daniel Douglas Home was known as a practised proponent of the levitating craft. In 1868 he was seen levitating out of a window on the third storey of a building. It was reported that he re-entered the building through another window on the same floor. Unlike the religious examples, Douglas Home did not enter a trance, and believed it just required a good deal of concentration. However, many people in the modern age believe the theories of levitation are best left to the engineers, designers and magicians in glamorous cabaret shows.

NEAR DEATH EXPERIENCES

MOST RELIGIONS AGREE that when we die, we are going to face some kind of reckoning or judgement. However, so much of our lives are spent dealing with trivial day-to-day distractions that we often forget this. For some people, a truly amazing phenomenon reasserts their priorities. It is a phenomenon that takes them beyond the shroud of life, to the very edges of the next dimension where they leave their mortal bodies and are shown the error of their ways. It is a phenomenon characterised by a dark tunnel, a shining light at the end, and extreme feelings of serendipity or fear. These are Near Death Experiences.

Near death experiences are reported by people who have been, at some stage, physically and medically dead – that is to say, they show no vital signs of life. It is normally experienced by heart attack sufferers, overdosed drug users, and people who have attempted suicide. Some estimates suggest that over ten million people in the United States have had personal experiences of near death experiences, so it is hardly a select phenomenon.

Although no two near death experiences are the same, they do share some common qualities. Many people report that they feel as if they have risen out of their body. Often they look down upon the medical teams trying to bring them back to life. Indeed, many people who have had near death experiences can even state exactly what happened, who said what, and which instruments were used to resuscitate them. Other experiences involve the person hovering above members of their family at the time of death.

Sometimes seeing their close relations is enough to force them to return to their mortal frames. But if they continue their near death experience, it is often reported that a feeling of sublime peace and joy sweeps over them. They find themselves in a dark tunnel with a beautiful white or golden light at the end of it. Sometimes they hear the voices of deceased loved ones, or even God, telling them to return to Earth. Some near death experiences involve an overview of the person's life, showing where things have gone wrong or need completing, and sometimes the person feels as though they have gained knowledge about the meaning of life. Whether by voluntary or involuntary means, they return to their bodies.

Not all near death experiences are so enjoyable, for there are some people who suffer horrific fear during their near death experience and see monsters or devils. What is largely universal is the effect of the experience on the person; they often instigate massive, life-changing decisions as a result. People review what is important in their life, and find new happiness from simple things. Many do voluntary work, or become teachers or lecturers. Those who do not chose to show their commitment to serving people publicly frequently reveal a new approach to life, and often become more pleasant, sympathetic and understanding.

In 2001, The Lancet medical journal published a report of a 13-year study into near death experiences that occurred in Dutch hospitals. The investigation was conducted by cardiologist Pim van Lommel, and was unique in that it questioned 344 patients immediately after they had been resuscitated. It was established that the patients' brains had no flow of blood, and so would have ceased to operate, yet 18% of those questioned had some memory of events during the time they were technically dead.

The researchers also found that 12% had a deep experience – that is, an out-of-body, bright light, or meeting of dead relatives type of phenomenon. The most impressive part was that the details of their experiences stayed precisely exact, even when they were re-interviewed two and eight years later. It was also seen that those who had near death experiences reprioritised, and became noticeably more appreciative of life, when compared to non- near death experience flat-liners. Near death experience sufferers also had a radically declined fear of death.

Some in the medical profession consider the accounts to be products of fantasy, false memory or confused consciousness. This view does a disservice to the huge numbers of people who genuinely feel they have had these moments; their reported near death experiences are just a sample – it has to be pointed out that many who had near death experiences in the past failed to come forward for fear of ridicule.

Do these experiences mean there really is an after-life? There is no scientific proof, although many near death experience sufferers will slip into death without fear when the time comes again. For them, it is not a step into the unknown.

OUIJA BOARDS

OUIJA BOARDS ARE known to teenagers across the world as the easiest way to create spooky, hair-raising experiences. Most people see them as a toy, something to play with. The fact that they were even mass-produced by games companies only adds to the 'harmless fun' factor. However, many expert mediums believe they should not be approached with such a nonchalant attitude. They say that countless people end up in dire straits simply from fooling around with Ouija boards; some experience mental breakdowns or relationships disintegrating, some end up possessed by spirits and some are even driven to suicide.

Nobody is precisely sure when the first Ouija board was made, but it seems that similar types of apparatus have been around for well over a century. The board itself consists of the letters of the alphabet, the numbers zero to nine, and the words 'yes' and 'no'. In fact, the name Ouija comes from the words for 'Yes' in French and German. The people using the board all gently touch a pointer which slides around the board, forming words that answer the questions asked by the sitters.

Contact with the spirits, or a cheap party game?

Officially, manufacturers of the boards say they works by tapping into the collective sub-conscious, but the item is generally regarded as a way to talk to spirits. Indeed, during the Second World War sales of the board peaked as people tried to contact loved ones lost in battle. The Ouija board then had a resurgence in the 1960s during the days of heightened spiritual interest. It was overtly marketed as a game, but media stories questioning the effect of the board on people's emotional, spiritual and psychological equilibrium led to the items being removed from high-street shops.

The dangers people face when using the board are obvious. If the sitters are trying to contact the spirit world, then they are probably dealing with something about which they know nothing. Just from a common sense point of view, there are dangers involved similar to modern forms of communication; you never know exactly who you are talking with, no matter what they tell you. It is claimed that especially mischievous or evil spirits try to contact people who are using Ouija boards without any clear idea of what they are doing. But, like modern technology, viewed and operated in the correct, careful way, people can have a lot of enjoyment.

Experts are particularly keen to warn people of nervous dispositions, who may be susceptible to unhealthy suggestion, to stay away from Ouija boards. There have been reports of extreme activity during sessions, with inanimate objects moving independently and lights flicking on and off. There is also no scientific proof to say exactly what is causing the words to be spelt out. If people really want to try contacting the spirit world it is probably advisable to visit a reputable medium who can guide and control sessions.

However, there are some Ouija board experiences that actually prove to be life-changing successes. Many of the established mediums began their careers using Ouija boards, and there is a strong argument that the boards help you become more sensitive and appreciative of the spirit world. One

such case happened in 1913 to Pearl Curran, a housewife from St Louis. Curran was dabbling with a friend's board when a spirit supposedly called Patience Worth contacted her. Curran and this entity progressed and she started to practise automatic writing, resulting in the production of over a million words of poetry, drama and fiction.

Of course there was always the possibility that Curran was a naturally gifted writer and just pretended a spirit had initiated the writing. She may even have been the unwitting reincarnation of Patience Worth. In either case, the prose was of a good enough quality to be published and receive substantial acclaim from readers.

However, not all experiences have this result. Whatever intellect is being harnessed, the fact is that with Ouija boards, like life in general, it is best to be careful with things you know little about.

POLTERGEISTS

IN GERMAN, THE WORD 'poltergeist' means 'noisy ghost.' It is an apt title, because of all paranormal activity, poltergeists are the most physical, forceful and frightening. They can make objects fly across the room, items shake, and strange and loud noises be heard. Often they are dangerous, and can leave people in a state of trauma. The most intriguing aspect of poltergeists is that they are actually caused by human predicaments and mental powers. In fact, they are such a well-studied and established phenomenon that science actually takes an active and interested role in researching them.

A haunting, and our traditional concept of a ghost, usually involves the lost soul of a

deceased person who is spiritually still in the same place where they lived or died. It is as if they have not realised their time has passed, and they are indiscriminate to whom they appear. Indeed, it is generally perceived that ghosts do not even realise the modern world is happening around them. Poltergeists, on the other hand, do react, disruptively, with their environment. Their disturbances can begin and end abruptly, and they have a very real, intrusive relationship with the people close by. Also, unlike traditional hauntings, it is believed they actually need a human to be the catalyst, or agent, for their activity.

This agent is crucial for poltergeist

Poltergeists – the word is the German for 'restless spirit' – are often thought to be the ghosts of children.

occurrences. Indeed, experts believe the agent is actually the root cause. It is understood that any type of person can be an agent, but there seems to be a particular susceptibility to poltergeist activity with young women. Although many agents are stable, balanced individuals with no control over the poltergeist, it is widely recognised that some agents have some deep-seated mental difficulties. It has been discovered that extreme states of anxiety, depression, hysteria, anger, schizophrenia and emotional fatigue are all powerful catalysts for poltergeist activity. Similarly, highly stressed individuals, or those with epilepsy, are regularly found to be poltergeist agents. The resultant events only serve to heighten any problems the agent has.

The symptoms of poltergeist disturbances are initially banging or knocking noises, awful smells, inexplicable lights, flying or moving objects and electrical equipment failures. As time passes by, if the cause is not sorted, the activity becomes more and more extreme. Experts are sincere when they believe poltergeists are dangerous both physically and mentally. They say that a person cannot run or move to escape from the poltergeist, that because the agent is responsible for its disturbances, it follows them. More advanced poltergeist activity involves unexplained dripping water, random fires igniting and vague apparitions appearing. Poltergeist activity is noticed and experienced by everyone in the room, and the disturbance is genuine physical activity, not imagined events.

As poltergeists have been studied for decades, scientists and experts have reached some conclusions. Many believe these strange events are caused by the agent releasing psychokinetic energy in an attempt to relieve stress. Psychokenisis is the idea of 'mind over matter' energy, and people are understood to expel huge amounts of it when under pressure. The actual activity that occurs is also symbolic of the problem. For example, some agents who feel intense guilt inspire a poltergeist to beat them and end up physically bruised all over. If an agent is incredibly angry with someone, then it will be their property that is thrown across the room and smashed by psychokinetic power. In almost all cases, the agent is as scared as everyone else, and does not realise that they are causing these events.

Experts agree that poltergeist activity is possible to solve, and many strongly suggest that those who experience it should seek help immediately. Whether the help comes from a priest or a psychologist, it is clear that poltergeist agents have an incredible power running loose that needs to be tamed. Once the cause is addressed, or even simply when the agent realises that they are the root of the disturbances, activity often stops. As with many paranormal experiences, the horror of poltergeists is not created by some unseen beast or phantom, but by the inexplicable power of the human mind.

PREMONITIONS

RESEARCHERS HAVE REVEALED that most premonitions predict events likely to happen within a very short space of time. They believe that women are more susceptible, or at least most ready to admit having them, but premonitions can be experienced by almost anyone. People who regularly experience premonitions can often determine how long the time delay between the dream and the ensuing reality is. For example, on 15th September 1981, Barbara Garwell had a dream involving the shooting of important Middle Eastern men at a stadium. She knew her premonition would take 21 days to show effect, and on the 6th of October, President Anwar Sadat was murdered at a mass commemoration.

Other versions of the phenomenon have arisen in equally strange ways. There is a theory that mortally important events can trigger mass premonitions where many people in the affected community foresee an impending tragedy or disaster. Perhaps the most striking of these happened at the Marfa colliery in Port Talbot, Wales. One day in 1890 over half of the miners in the town failed to turn up for work because of a general disquiet and feeling of foreboding. Some people even reported the 'smell of death' drifting up from the mine. In total, 87 miners went down to work that day, but a massive accident in the heart of the colliery meant none survived. A similar phenomenon was said to have been experienced by many passengers shortly before boarding the Titanic.

Without doubt, the largest modern source of premonition stories has been the World Trade Centre attack on 11th September 2001. Indeed, this event alone has initiated a massive resurgence in the belief of psychic forewarnings. There have been remarkable stories of artists and creative people including the disaster in works composed before the fateful day.

Charles Burwell III, a painter and self-confessed non-psychic, composed an unusual image between spring and September 2000. The picture showed a calamity in a city of large pillars, but it caused Burwell so much distress that he did not finish it. In a similar case, intelligence agents investigated an Egyptian calendar printed in May 2001. On the page for September, the decorative picture seemed to depict a passenger plane crashing into tall buildings with Manhattan and the Statue of Liberty in the distance behind. If, as it seems, some of the hijackers were not aware of what was to unfold, it seems highly unlikely that the information was passed on to calendar manufacturers.

The case of the World Trade Centre has caused many premonition investigators to ask for individual experiences n the run-up to the disaster. The British Society for Psychical Research has started a confidential website for people to log any experiences about the World Trade Centre attack, or any other premonition, whether it has come to pass or not. This idea of a predictions catalogue is not new; a British Premonitions Bureau was originally set up in 1957. In the

Foretelling the future with the aid of a chicken. Why poultry is ascribed such powers is perhaps more of a mystery than clairvoyancy itself.

first year, over a thousand premonitions were filed, and although they had some proven forewarnings, the bureau was shut down within a few years. The concept does throw up some interesting logical questions. Those who promote it say that if people logged their ideas, and the public took notice, it could help avoid terrible disasters. If all warnings were heeded, and we all stayed at home, all of the time, there would certainly be no terrible accidents. But we would also never know how accurate any premonitions actually were.

Many doubts about the integrity of premonitions are based on explanations of logic. Numerous experts believe a fair proportion of premonitions are created by environment, custom, people's nature and probable possibilities. Instinct, intuition and common sense can be just as effective as mystical messages. Other theories state that sheer chance suggests many realistic dreams will come true, at least in part at some point in time. Dr Richard Wiseman advanced a theory which stated that, if somebody dreams about a plane crash and they then look hard enough, within a reasonably short space of time a suitably similar event will appear in the media. Air crash experts, however, dispute this and point to the overall low number of fatal passenger airline incidents.

Like many mysteries, people can interpret events in whatever way suits them, but there are still some impressive cases of premonitions. If only we could be warned before the event, then many sceptics would be truly silenced.

REINCARNATION

How do some children have the ability to speak in dialects and remember details of events that happened years before their birth? Reincarnation is the belief that the soul of a person returns to Earth after death and takes residency in a new body. It is a belief borne in the philosophies of Eastern religions and the Karmic laws of nature. Such is the level of complete conviction that some Buddhist holy men even believe it is a crime to kill any living creature for fear that it is a loved one returned. These ways of the mystical East are increasingly finding favour in our normally sceptical societies, and many people now purposely search for details of their past lives through hypnotic regression.

Christianity, and particularly the Roman Catholic Church, see reincarnation as heresy, although many branches of religion are open to the possibility. The central theme of the Buddhist religion, for example, relies on reincarnation. Buddha himself taught that the point of reincarnation depends on the quality of the preceding life. This is the idea of Karma, and the belief that one's actions are repaid in equal kind. Buddhists believe that reincarnation is needed to understand the world and achieve enlightenment. Once this is achieved, the soul will break the chain of reincarnation, attaining a state of nirvana or spiritual heaven.

The current trends for therapy and counselling in the Western world have also increased interest in the phenomenon of reincarnation. Problems such as irrational fears, recurring nightmares and inexplicable health problems are said to be caused by shadow memories of former lives. To solve these difficulties, people often undergo hypnosis to experience regression to find details of past lives. Experts believe that, in the wrong therapist's hands, these processes can be unhelpful, and a combination of latent imagination and leading questions can produce quite fanciful results.

Details of past lives can appear completely unsolicited. Experiences such as spontaneous recall, where the person suddenly see an ultra real 'daydream,' or triggered recall, where an external factor in the physical world acts as a catalyst for the memory, are both common examples of this. It is suggested that anybody interested in discovering their own past memories actually undertake a long course of meditation or yoga. Although the process does not yield immediate results, and may take years to develop, the individual retains self-control and also achieves a higher state of mystical and spiritual wellbeing.

As the subject of reincarnation gains more and more acceptance, an increasing amount of verified cases are being reported. One of the most famous was that of the movie star Glenn Ford. Under hypnosis, Ford claimed to remember five previous lives, the most impressive of which was as a French cavalryman during the reign of Louis XIV. Despite the fact that Ford only knew a few rudimentary phrases in French, under hypnosis he was able to speak fluently in a language that was later discovered to be a particular Parisian dialect from the seventeenth century. This is quite astounding evidence, but many sceptics still claim that these sort of 'memories' can be created by sub-conscious dreaming.

Children's recounts of past lives often provide the most amazing and most reliable proof of reincarnation, as they are not corrupted with the notion of reincarnation or false histories. Dr Ian Stevenson, a leading researcher in this field, has written about many fascinating cases. One such incident involved an Indiana girl called Swarnlata Mishra.

In 1951, when Swarnlata was three, she started giving details about a woman called Biya Pathak who had lived in the Katni, over a hundred miles away from Swarnlata's family home in Pradesh. The young girl revealed that Pathak had two sons and had died in 1939 of a 'pain in her throat.' She described and positioned Biya's home and seemed to remember more and more as time passed by. Eventually, Biya's family were tracked down and came to visit Swarnlata to test her knowledge. She immediately recognised all the correct relations of Biya, calling them by their nicknames and treating them just as Biya would have. Over the years she developed a close relationship with the Pathak's, and both families now accept that Swarnlata is Biya returned. When Swarnlata's father, Sri Mishra decided to chose a husband for her, he even consulted the Pathak family. Stories like this that affect people so personally suggest reincarnation really is a reality.

REMOTE VIEWING

REMOTE VIEWING IS one of the most verifiable of all human paranormal abilities. It allows 'viewers' the power to see and experience situations and places separated from them by distance and time. Using naturally inherent psychic talents, known as psi, the viewer then records details of what he or she has seen. Many enthusiasts say it is an acquirable craft rather than some divine gift and that, whereas many so-called psychic powers now have unfortunate connotations of con-men and tricksters, remote viewing, or RV, began as a scientific experiment and is used by police, military and large corporate organisations.

Many companies now offer remote viewing tutorials and promise that anyone can understand and control this ability with practise and a good teacher. Unlike other psi powers such as clairvoyance, remote viewing is conducted under strict controls. Viewers are not allowed to know anything of their target other than the detail that instigates the search. It might be a photograph or a co-ordinate on which the viewer then trains their thoughts following a scripted format. The viewer operates in a quiet room, often going into a trance-like state, and sometimes has a companion who helps direct them. Unlike an out-of-body phenomenon, the viewer always knows where they really are. They still feel and experience all aspects of their target.

The creator of remote viewing was an

American artist and paranormal student called Ingo Swann. Swann had taken aspects of previous psychic experiments and formed a new technique, which was tested by scientists at the American Society for Psychological Research. In these tests, he was able to accurately describe in detail the weather in different US cities. In 1972 Swann was introduced to Dr Hal Puthoff, a physicist at the Stanford Research Institute in California. The two conducted further experiments and were subsequently approached by the CIA. The department approached Puthoff with some tasks it wanted his team to look at, and were impressed with the results.

At the time, American intelligence experts were becoming increasingly worried about reports coming from Russia that Soviet authorities were spending vast sums on paranormal activities. The CIA had become aware that Communist scientists were developing psychic warfare capabilities including 'psychic spies.' Initially, Puthoff's programme was used to test the feasibility of this. But as remote viewing produced more accurate and detailed results, the use of viewers in intelligence gathering roles was explored, and various military and intelligence agencies developed their own branches of the remote viewing programme.

The potential of Swann's work grew immensely, and rather than just using people who already had a demonstrable psychic ability, he recruited normal, non-psychic civilians. In 1991 the entire US programme was renamed the 'Star Gate' project. With the end of the Cold War, viewers were used to collect intelligence against a broad range of targets, including drug dealers, tyrants and terrorists. Swann had also developed an effective new technique called Co-ordinate or Controlled Remote Viewing, which actually directed viewers to their targets. In 1995 the US Congress decided that the remote viewing programme be given back to the CIA, who then commissioned an unfavourable report. The team was disbanded and many of the military viewers have gone on to offer their services privately with a few even receiving contracts from the US intelligence agencies to work in a freelance capacity.

Other nations have not been so quick to end their official psychic warfare divisions. The intelligence agencies of Russia, France and especially China continue to fund and study in-depth experiments. Many intelligence experts believe China has a select group of military 'Superpsychics.' Their programme is said to be highly advanced, even to the point of recruiting and training particularly talented psychic children.

More peaceful uses of remote viewing have been adopted by large corporations, and controlled, scientific research in civilian universities has come to some staggering conclusions – particularly talented viewers are said to achieve results with odds of over 100 billion to one. As the subject has become more widely available in the public domain, former members of the US military involved in the project have spoken out; even former president Jimmy Carter has recounted tales of remote viewing. He reports having once met a female viewer who was looking for a lost aircraft, 'She went into a trance. And while she was in the trance, she gave us some latitude and longitude figures. We focused our satellite cameras on that point, and the lost plane was there.' With testimonies like this there can be little doubt that remote viewing is a genuine phenomenon.

SÉANCES

SÉANCES ARE AN age-old way for the living to communicate with the dead. The popular image of a group sitting round a table, holding hands, with the room lights flickering, is a little over-dramatic, but not so far from the truth. Many people believe the collective energy of a number of participants or 'sitters' helps attract spirits. Generally, there should also be an experienced medium, who channels the messages and helps control the sitting.

Although séances had a reputation for trickery and fraudulent practices in the past, a talented and honest medium can make them an interesting way to explore contacting spirits.

Before a séance can begin, it is necessary to have a particular spirit, which the sitters want to reach in mind. It also helps if a relative, or someone who had known the spirit in their lifetime, is part of the group – this is a reason why attempts by people to

Is there anybody there? A séance in progress.

147

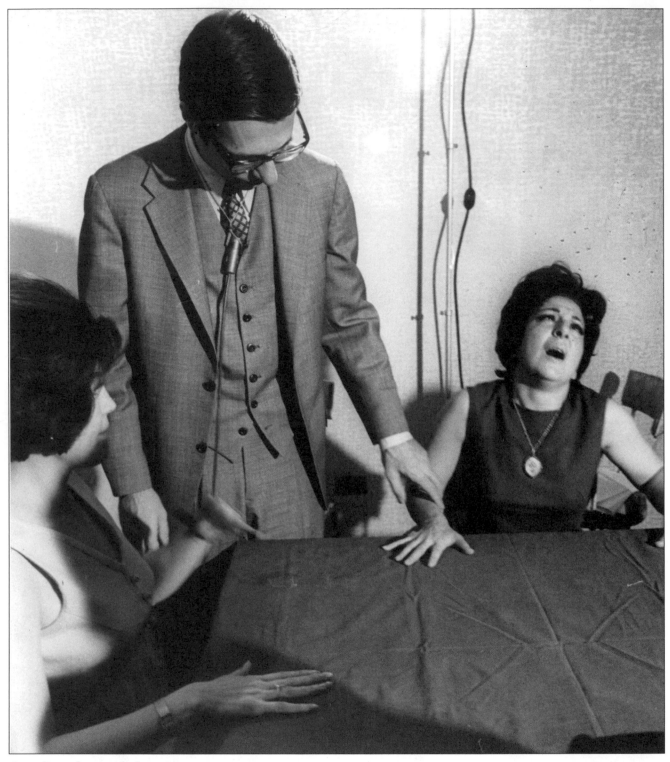

A medium chats with the spirits.

contact ghosts of Elvis and the like are unsuccessful. The contact spirit will often know that the séance is going to happen, and will want to talk. The room must be a peaceful environment, and the sitters must be comfortable and undisturbed. They should then sit in a circle, or around a table, and may hold hands if they wish although that is not essential. Together, they mentally call the spirit they are searching for.

Often the medium enters a trance-like state and will begin channelling messages from the spirit world. Sometimes this coincides with odd physical experiences, such as a cool breeze wafting through, strange perfumes, or a tickling sensation. Often sitters also feel a slight pain corresponding to how the spirit died – for example, a chest pain is felt with a spirit who died of a heart attack. Hopefully, the medium finds the spirit the sitters have asked for, but other spirits are sometimes also eager to chat. The medium leads the discussion, and allows it to continue for as long as the sitters want.

With a professional psychic, the chances of having a bad experience are very slim, and many people feel that it acts as a significant healing process for both the bereaved and the deceased.

SPONTANEOUS HUMAN COMBUSTION

THE MERE NOTION that a human being has the potential to burst into flames without the help of an external ignition source seems too ridiculous for study. Surely there is nothing inside the body that could create such a reaction? And yet, for over three hundred years, reliable records have testified to a phenomenon where people, with no prior warning or exposure to naked flames, simply combust in a fit of intense heat. All that is left is a pile of ash and perhaps a random charred limb. The fact that no damage ever seems to be done to nearby textiles leaves experts perplexed. This inexplicable phenomenon is called spontaneous human combustion.

Many of those who are attacked by spontaneous human combustion, or SHC, are often simply sitting in a chair when the event affects them. At one time, it was thought many subjects were alcoholics, and one old theory behind spontaneous human combustion was that it was caused by a chemical reaction brought on by alcohol in the blood and a fit of geriatric pique. This is now largely discredited, but there are some common qualities in occurrences of spontaneous human combustion. Generally, it is the trunk of the body that is most severely burnt, and frequently a couple of smouldering, blackened feet are found where the person should have been. Similarly, arms, skulls and even spinal cords are often the only distinguishable remains.

The actual damage to the bodies affected by spontaneous human combustion appears to be created by a heat more intense than even that of a crematorium. A universal theme of spontaneous human combustion occurrences is that despite this extreme temperature – which experts believe is probably around 600°C – objects or material around the person are not destroyed, although obviously their clothing is burnt, and sometimes there is a patch of scorched carpet where their feet would have been. In one case, a woman died following an incidence of spontaneous human combustion in bed and the sheets were not even marked. However, occasionally a greasy, sooty dust is found on ceilings and walls nearby.

Spontaneous human combustion was recorded in 1673 by a Frenchman, James Dupont, who studied a selection of cases of the phenomenon in his book, De Incendiis Corporis Humani Spontaneis. Dupont's interest in the subject was initially aroused by the Nicolle Millet court case. In this instance, a man was found not guilty of murdering his wife because the jury ruled that she had actually suffered an attack of spontaneous human combustion. From the late seventeenth century the idea of spontaneous human combustion gained credence and acceptance in popular life. Indeed, Charles Dickens used the phenomenon as the reason of death for a character called Krook in his 1852 novel, Bleak House.

The most celebrated case of spontaneous human combustion happened on 2nd July 1951 to a 67-year-old pensioner from Florida, USA called Mary Reeser. The only parts of Reeser's body to be found were her skull, which had shrunk to the size of a baseball, her spinal column, her left foot, and a pile of ash still in her armchair. The authorities declared she had died in a normal household fire, but no part of her apartment, including cotton sheets and a pile of newspapers left nearby, was damaged.

A similar event occurred recently in France. On 17th November 1998, the few remains of a 67-year-old woman called Gisele were found in her farmhouse near Honfleur. Only a pile of ashes and her slippered left foot were discovered. In this case, even the wheelchair in which she was sitting had disintegrated, although the rest of her farmhouse stood untouched by fire.

In such cases, police investigators can only take a guess or choose the most plausible option given the seemingly inconsistent facts. Spontaneous human combustion investigators themselves have no satisfactory explanations. The alcoholism and anger mixture has no scientific grounding and the suggestion that it is caused by excessive fat deposits that catch alight is also dismissed, whilst the idea that spontaneous human combustion is caused by some error in the body's electrical system is unverifiable.

Perhaps the most acceptable explanation for the time being is that spontaneous human combustion is caused by an Act of God. Although that can have no easily studied scientific basis, for now it is the most reassuring answer to a mystery that truly is inexplicable.

PUZZLING PEOPLE AND ENIGMATIC ENTITIES

Anastasia/Anna Anderson

In February 1920, two years after the execution of the Russian Czar and his family, a young woman attempted suicide by jumping off a bridge in Berlin. She was rescued, but when she arrived at hospital she had no proof of identity on her and would not reveal her name. The hospital sent her to an insane asylum where she was recognised as the Czar's daughter, Grand Duchess Tatiana. The woman denied that she was Tatiana, but over time revealed that she was actually his other daughter, the Duchess Anastasia. She explained that the bayonets of the Communist death squad soldiers had been blunt and she had survived the assassination attempt. One of the soldiers who came to remove the bodies noticed that she was still alive and spirited her away to Romania. She had come to Berlin to find her aunt, Princess Irene, but fear of not being recognised led to her taking such desperate measures. The woman adopted the name Anna Anderson, and spent much of her life trying to prove she was Anastasia.

When news of her appearance first spread, one of Alexandra's ladies-in-waiting visited the hospital, but Anderson kept her head covered with blankets so the woman declared her a fake. Similarly, Princess Irene met Anderson and refuted her claims, although in private it is said she was not so sure, and her son Sigismund actually declared that he thought Anderson was

Princess Anastasia before the assassination.

Anastasia. The community of European monarchies were generally undecided. The Czar's mistress, Mathilde Kschessinka, believed Anderson was the young princess,

Happy families: the Tsar's people, however, were less happy with his rule of the country.

and Pierre Guillard, Anastasia's former tutor, also initially declared his support before changing his mind. The family of another court employee – the monarch's doctor Eugene Botkin – were utterly convinced of Anderson's true royal lineage, particularly as she could talk in detail about personal correspondences between the young princesses and Botkin's children.

In attitude, Anderson certainly behaved like a princess. She was said to be demanding and arrogant, and could be consumed by fits of rage. She spoke excellent English, French and German, and could fully understand Russian although she refused to speak it. She also had scars on her body that matched her execution claims, and facial experts argued that she looked very similar to Anastasia. She had similar physical deformities to the young princess, and calligraphic experts said their handwriting was identical. Anderson was also said to have an amazing knowledge of royal affairs. She revealed that Anastasia's uncle, Grand

Duke Ernst of Hesse, had secretly visited the Russian monarchy in 1916 when the two families had actually been at war. This fact was only categorically proven in 1966, but Ernst always denied the claims.

It has been suggested that Ernst starting circulating another theory which was that Anderson was actually a Polish factory worker named Franziska Schanzkowski. People started to claim that Schanzkowski disappeared only a day before Anderson's appearance in Berlin. It was said that Anderson's scars had arisen from a time when Schanzkowski had dropped a live grenade whilst working at an armaments factory. However, Anderson was small and frail, whereas Schanzkowski was raised on a farm and supposedly had a very stocky build. Anderson continually tried to prove her heritage, but she never succeeded conclusively in a court of law. In late 1968 she married a wealthy American called John Manahan, and she died of pneumonia in 1984. Her body was cremated, but advances in DNA testing meant her death was not the end of the saga.

In 1991, the remains of eight people were found in Siberia. Forensic testing suggests the corpses of Nicholas, Alexandra and three of their children were among the bodies. British scientists compared their DNA with samples of Anderson's hair, and found no match. However, Anderson did seem to have extremely similar DNA results to blood samples taken from the grand-nephew of Franziska Schanzkowski. So it appears the

The survivor of the massacre of the Russian royal family, or a Polish factory worker named Franziska?

mystery of Anna Anderson has been put to rest. Except for one thing. When Russian authorities uncovered the royal bodies in 1991, two corpses were missing. One was the Czar's son Alexei. The other was his youngest daughter, Anastasia.

COMTE DE SAINT-GERMAIN

THE MYSTERIOUS FIGURE we now know as the Comte de Saint-Germain was first witnessed in 1710 under the name the Marquis de Montferrat. Seen in Venice by a musician named Rameau and a Parisian socialite called Madam de Gergy, he had the appearance of a man between 40 and 50 years of age. It was an appearance he would hold all his life, and he would only officially die in 1784. However, many people believe he never actually passed away. To them, this enigmatic character has become known as 'Saint-Germain the Deathless.'

Saint-Germain's provenance was never revealed, not even by those he had taken into his confidence. For his entire life he looked like a middle-aged, strongly built man of average height. He was an amazing raconteur with incredible stories, and had some impressive talents. He could create fantastic jewels, had a complete understanding of music and art, and was able to provide people with potions which he claimed were the elixir of youth. He was never seen to eat or drink, but he enjoyed the company of women and mixed with the aristocracy. He never seemed to age.

His great period of celebrity was in Paris between 1750 and 1760. His main role was that of spy for King Louis XV. However, his friendship with the king created many enemies within the French government and he was forced to flee to England. He resurfaced in Russia under the name General Soltikov and played a major role in the 1762 revolution. At the start of Louis XVI's reign

One of the few portraits to show the mysterious Comte de Saint-Germain.

he reappeared in Paris and, through an old friend, the Countesse d'Adhemar, he issued a warning to Queen Marie Antoinette of the dangers that were building for the French monarchy. Saint-Germain tried to see the king personally, but the police were ordered to capture the Comte by the king's minister. Again, Saint-Germain simply disappeared.

He apparently sought refuge at the castle of Count Charles of Hesse Cassel in the Duchy of Schlesing, Austria. It was said that he revealed many of his secrets to the count, but by 1784 Saint-Germain had simply grown bored of life and died. However, there is no official record of his death, and no tombstone bearing his name. He left all his papers, many of which concerned freemasonry, to the count, but like Louis XV, Charles never revealed anything about Saint-Germain's real history. Indeed, even though he claimed to be sad that Saint-Germain had died, many commentators have suggested he did not appear so upset, and there is a theory that he may have been privy to a staged death.

Certainly, further reports of Saint-Germain have been recorded. In 1786 he met the Empress of Russia, and in 1788 he was apparently the official French representative at the World Convention of Freemasons. The Countess of d'Adhemar said she had met her old friend in 1789, 1815 and 1821, and that each time he looked no older than her memory of him. It is said that he continued to have an influence on secret societies and may even have been a guiding light of the Rosicrucians.

So who was the strange character? Parisians who disliked him said he was the son of a Portuguese Jew named Aymar, or an Alsatian Jew called Wolff. However, the general feeling at the time was that he was the natural son of Spain's Charles II's widow, Marie de Neubourg. A more recent study has suggested that he may actually have been one of the sons of Prince Francis Racoczi II of Transylvania. The prince gave his children to the Emperor of Austria to bring up, but one of them was said to have died at a young age. It is now considered that this child may have, in fact, been raised by a family in the little village of San Germano in Italy. This would account for how he assumed the name the Comte de Saint-Germain.

However, some people, particularly those involved with the Theosophy movement, believe Saint-Germain may have been one of the 'great masters', sent to show developed men the errors of their ways. They believe he may be still wandering the Earth, waiting for the right time to reappear and counsel Man through troubled waters. Until then, however, the enigmatic figure known as the Comte de Saint-Germain will remain a mystery.

DRACULA

EASTERN EUROPE OF THE Middle Ages was a turbulent place. The great Hungarian nation was its first line of defence against Ottoman forces, and the individual states that happened to be placed in 'No-man's land' between the two suffered terrible unrest. It was enough to inspire Bram Stoker to write his most famous novel, although people now question which figure during this unstable period was the greatest influence on the writer. Only one name truly stands out – the real, terrible man known as Dracula.

Walachia, now part of Romania, was a Hungarian province ruled by Prince Mircea the Old until 1418. In around 1390, Mircea had an illegitimate son named Vlad who was given away to be brought up in the court of

Hungary's King Sigismund. When Mircea died, Vlad was not given control of Walachia, but he was made a Knight of the Order of the Dragon, a group set up to defend the Christian world from Turkish rule. Vlad was soon given the name 'Dracul,' meaning 'dragon,' and was made governor of Transylvania.

Dracul had three sons. The first, named after his father Mircea, was born in 1443, with the next two called Vlad and Radu. Dracul gathered an army and took back his family's traditional seat of power in Walachia, although he only succeeded with the help of old enemy Turkey. As a sign of his loyalty, sent Vlad and Radu to live in Adrianople, the seat of the Ottoman Empire.

In 1447 Dracul and Mircea were killed, and a Hungarian government again ruled Walachia. This situation made Turkey uncomfortable, so in 1448 they decided to arm the seventeen-year-old Vlad who was known as the 'Son of Dragon,' or Dracula.

Over the years and battles the protagonists continued to swap sides, but by 1456 Dracula had reclaimed his throne in Walachia. He built a capital city at Tirgoviste and was pronounced Prince Vlad III. From the beginning, he realised that to survive he would have to be shown as utterly ruthless. Shortly after he was crowned prince, he invited destitute souls from the streets of his kingdom to a great feast at his castle. After the meal, he asked the assembled poor, frail

Woodcut of a vampire feeding on the blood of another victim.

and aged if they would 'like to be without cares, lacking nothing in the world?' When they all cried 'yes' he promptly boarded up the castle and set fire to it. He said there was little place in his society for people who would be a burden, and anybody who did not contribute to the community received scant sympathy.

If killing the infirm was a sign to the public, Dracula committed a similar action with Walachia's dignitaries. He had the older ones impaled, and sent the others to build a castle at Poenari, a mountainous area 50 miles away. In their place, Dracula organised his own set of nobles to confirm his power. His evil knew no bounds, and he particularly enjoyed watching people die after being hoisted on a sharpened pole. His people called him Vlad Tepes meaning 'Vlad the Impaler' and the Turkish knew him as Kaziglu Boy or the 'Impaler Prince.' He murdered cheating wives, fraudulent merchants, anybody who committed any crime. Often he would have many victims impaled at the same time, but he also enjoyed skinning and boiling people alive. He killed children and the old, and put their bodies on public display to warn would-be

miscreants. It is said that 20,000 dead bodies hung from the walls of Tirgoviste, and by the end of his reign he had killed around 50,000 people.

In 1462 when Walachia was attacked by the Turks, led by Dracula's younger brother Rada, Dracula went into exile in Hungary. In 1476, with Radu dead of syphilis and another prince on Walachia's throne, Dracula attempted to regain his rightful home. He succeeded, but in December 1476 was killed during another Turkish attack. The Ottoman sultan impaled Dracula's head and had it displayed in Constantinople as evidence of his death. His body was said to have been buried as an island monastery called Snagov, although investigative digs in 1931 were unable to find the coffin. It is one final mystery to the Dracula story.

Some proof of his reign does remain though. His fortress in the hills of Poenari stands today as a popular tourist destination, and there are also ruins of his palace at Tirgoviste. More important than any physical heritage is his memory in the mind of the Romanian people. But whether his life is the sole inspiration behind Bram Stoker's story or not, we shall never know.

Jack the Ripper

In 1888, the world's most famous serial killer stalked the dark, grimy streets of London's East End. 'Jack the Ripper' was the original celebrity mass-murderer, and set a trend for homicidal maniacs which seems to grow with each year. The fear surrounding the recent Washington sniper incidents, for example, has many similarities with the terror created by this forefather of death-dealing criminals. In these types of cases, the impact of the crime is heightened by the

mystery surrounding the actual killer's identity. Unlike many of his modern age copyists, Jack the Ripper was not caught or even named, and to this day it has never been conclusively proven who he really was.

London's Whitechapel district was known as one of the poorest areas of the city, and at the time, was home to over a thousand prostitutes. It was also the area which would become the focus of the Ripper's attacks. His reign of terror officially began in the opening

Jack the Ripper strikes again in this contemporary illustration. Was he the royal physician, or even royal himself?

hours of 31st August 1888, when a market porter spotted a woman lying in a doorway on Buck's Row in Whitechapel. Rather than approach the woman, the porter went to find the beat policeman. When he arrived, he found the woman's throat had been deeply cut and a medical examination later revealed her body had been mutilated. Her identity was also discovered: she was Mary Ann Nichols, known as Polly, a 42 year-old prostitute.

Barely a week later, at 6am on 8th September, the body of another woman was found in Hanbury Street, near Buck's Row. She was Annie Chapman, a 45-year-old prostitute whose head had been almost entirely severed from her neck; she had also been disembowelled.

Annie Chapman, victim of the Ripper.

Fear was beginning to spread throughout the community. For the first time in history, the people had a literate public and a scrutinising press, who were putting the police under a new sort of pressure. Not only were the police there to protect the people of London, they also had to cope with the novel stress of proving their own competence. Just as in modern mass murder cases, the effect of supposition, myths and rumours in newspaper coverage led to a great deal of anxiety.

By the time the Ripper struck again, the Whitechapel area was interested in only one thing. The Ripper did not disappoint. In the dark early hours of 30th September a costume jewellery salesman arrived home in Berners Street, where he discovered the body of Elizabeth Stride, a prostitute who had had her throat slit. As police rushed to the scene and searched the nearby streets, the Ripper

made off to Mitre Square, in the City of London, and killed Catharine Eddowes. Although the earlier victim had not been mutilated, many believe the Ripper had been interrupted during this procedure. Eddowes' remains were not so well preserved and she was found disembowelled.

This night become known as the 'double event,' and was the focus of many letters sent into the police. Although most came from members of the public offering advice, some purported to come from the Ripper himself and were given more credence than others. One dated 28th September goaded and teased the police, and was the origin of the name Jack the Ripper, which was how the sender signed off. The second was a postcard dated 1st October and referred to the 'double event' of the night before. The third letter was posted a fortnight later and even included a section of a kidney allegedly removed from Catharine Eddowes. Although the police, as in modern times, had to suspect that these correspondences came from a crank or a hoaxer, the kidney included in the third letter was shrivelled and diseased. An interesting fact is that not only was Eddowes an alcoholic, she also suffered from Bright's disease, and this organ displayed all the signs of being from such an afflicted body.

The police believed they had discovered a pattern to the killings the first occurred on 31st August, the second on 8th September, the third and fourth on 30th September. They believed the next would happen on the 8th of October, but in fact the Ripper did not strike for the whole of that month. His final official murder actually occurred on 9th November in Miller's Court, a building close to where the other killings had taken place. Another prostitute, 24-year-old Mary Jane Kelly was found by her landlord with her body utterly mutilated. This time, the murder had taken place inside, and the killer had had all night to dissect the corpse.

Although these five murders are all assigned to the Ripper, there is the possibility he may have killed two or three more woman in London around that time. However, the police were at a loss to find the real name of the man behind the crimes and employed a policy of information suppression to try to reassure the public. Despite this, Londoners were fully aware that police work was proving fruitless at obtaining a clear picture of the Ripper's identity. But some of those in the force did have their own theories, and many police doctors who examined the victims' bodies suggested the Ripper was likely to be someone with medical training. In 1894 the Chief Constable of the Metropolitan Police Force, Sir Melville Macnaghten, wrote a report which named Montague John Druitt, a barrister who committed suicide shortly after the Kelly murder, as the most likely suspect. However, at the time Macnaghten believed Druitt to be a trained doctor, which subsequent research proved to be false.

Macnaghten also named two more possible Rippers. One was Aaron Kosminski, a Polish Jew who lived in the Whitechapel area and was placed in an insane asylum in March 1889. Although one of the chief investigating officers, Robert Anderson, had a great belief in Kosminski's guilt, the Pole's behavioural records from his time in the asylum contain nothing to suggest he was homicidal. Macnaghten's final suspect, Michael Ostrog, was a Russian lunatic. Despite being a convicted criminal and possibly having some medical training, his behaviour under studied conditions also did not point to an ability for multiple murders. In recent years, Ripper investigators have considered Dr Francis Tumblety, an American doctor who fled London shortly after the murders. Despite thinking him a possible suspect, the Metropolitan Police at the time decided to rule him out of its enquires.

As with many mysteries, the identity of the Ripper has become the domain of conspiracy theorists. This has led to people from all walks of life – members of the monarchy, royal servants, high-ranking police officers, Russian spies and even crazed evangelists – being accused of holding the Ripper's identity. However, in the last few of years a study has been conducted by the crime writer Patricia Cornwell. She used $4million of her own money to investigate if there is a link between the Ripper and Walter Sickert, an impressionist painter who may have had connections with Whitechapel around the dates of the murders. Twenty years after the killings, he created a series of paintings that depicted dead and gruesomely mauled prostitutes. Cornwell has used modern technologies and intense examinations of his work, and is so convinced of Sickert's guilt that she is staking her reputation on him being the Ripper.

Modern Ripper investigators, just like the Victorian London police forces, fail to agree with each other. There were so many unsavoury characters roaming London at the time that almost any suspect could have been linked to the murders in some way. As the years blur the truth, so the plausibility of many different suspects increases, whilst the definitive proof needed to decide on one disappears in the fog of time.

Kaspar Hauser

On 26th May 1828, a strange, teenage boy stumbled up to the gates of Nuremberg. He had a strong build, light curly hair, a pale complexion, and moved as if he was drunk. A local shoemaker, Georg Weickmann, approached the boy to see who he was, but the lad only said, 'I would like to be a rider the way my father was.' He handed Weickmann an envelope addressed to the Captain of the fourth squadron of the sixth regiment of the Light Cavalry. The shoemaker took him to the captain, who opened the letter. It explained that the boy had been left with a poor labourer who had kept him locked inside all his life. But the boy was now ready to serve in the king's army.

The cavalry captain questioned the boy, but the only words he said were, 'don't know,' 'take me home,' and 'horse.' He could also write the name 'Kaspar Hauser.' In the end, the captain put the boy in the local prison but the jailer took pity on him. The jailer's children began to teach him to speak, write and draw. He seemed to have no concept of behaviour; had no facial expressions; could not understand the difference between men and women; was happy to sleep sitting up; acted like a baby or infant child and was particularly happy in the dark.

In July 1828 a local magistrate suggested to Nuremberg's authorities that it would be best for Hauser to be taken out of the jail and placed in the custody of George Friedrich Daumer, a university professor and psychologist. Daumer helped Hauser change into a normal young man, but also kept a record of the strange boy's behaviour. Daumer realised the extent of Hauser's amazing heightened senses. He could read in the dark, hear whispers from extreme distances and discern who was in a pitch black room simply by their smell. Unfortunately, as his awareness and education about the world around him increased, these extraordinary abilities waned.

By early 1829, Hauser had learnt enough to be able to write his autobiography. In it he revealed that he had been kept in a cell 7ft long, 4ft wide and 5ft high by a man whose face he never saw. He slept on a straw bed, and when he woke there would be water and bread for him to eat. Sometimes the water would taste odd, and he would pass out only to find himself cleaned and groomed, wearing with a fresh set of clothes when he awoke. One day the man came to Hauser's cell door with books and taught him to read a little, write his name, and repeat the rudimentary phrases he pronounced on his public arrival. The next day, Hauser and his captor began a three day journey which culminated in his appearance at Nuremberg.

Hauser's autobiography opened the door to a new terror. In October 1829 a stranger dressed in black came to Daumer's house and tried to kill Hauser with a knife. Lord Stanhope, an English aristocrat and friend of the ruling Baden family, then struck up a friendship with Hauser, and gained guardianship of the boy from the city of Nuremberg. Stanhope quickly lost interest and placed the boy in the town of Ansbach under the care of a Dr Meyer. Meyer disliked the boy and became a hard and mean-spirited tutor. On 14th December 1831, Hauser went to a local park to meet a man who had promised to reveal details about his mother's identity. They met, and the stranger motioned as if to give Hauser a wallet, but as the young man leant forward, he was stabbed in his side. He died three days later aged just 21.

The suspicion developed that Hauser was actually a Baden prince and son of Stephanie, Grand Duchess of Bavaria. Certainly many of the Bavarian aristocracy had such suspicions, and King Ludwig of Bavaria even wrote in his diary that Hauser was the 'rightful Grand Duke of Baden.' The theory is that Stephanie and Karl of Baden had Hauser in 1812, but Karl's stepmother, the Duchess of Hochberg, switched him at birth with a sickly peasant child. The ill baby soon passed away and subsequent boys sired by Karl with Stephanie also died young. Karl himself died in strange circumstances, and on his deathbed said he believed that he and his boys had been poisoned. Karl's throne then went to his stepbrother, the Duchess of Hochberg's son Leopold. It is an unprovable theory.

All we definitely know is that in a peaceful countryside churchyard there is a gravestone that reads:

'Here lies Kaspar Hauser, riddle of his time. His birth was unknown, his death mysterious.'

KING ARTHUR

THE LEGEND OF King Arthur states that he was born sometime in the fifth century AD. It is said that the great magician Merlin disguised Uther Pendragon, one of England's great warriors, to look like the Duke of Tintagel, the husband of Ingraine of Cornwall. Uther seduced Ingraine at Tintagel cottage, but the child they conceived was given away at birth. He was named Arthur and was raised completely unaware of his special lineage. When Uther died, the throne was empty. Merlin set a sword called Excaliber in rock and stated that only someone of a truly royal bloodline would be able to remove Excaliber from its fixed position. When the young Arthur was the only one able to do this, he was pronounce king. Eleven other British rulers rebelled against the young leader, but Arthur quashed their uprising and began a noble and glorious reign.

Arthur married Guinevere and assembled a group of courageous and honest knights at a kingdom seat in Camelot, in the Vale of Avalon. To avoid any sense of preference among the knights, Guinevere's father provided Arthur with the fabled Round Table. Together they had great victories over Saxon invaders and the Roman Empire. Arthur is even said to have become Emperor himself and set about on a search for the Holy Grail. However, during this time one of Arthur's most trusted knights, Lancelot, had an affair with Guinevere.

This marked the beginning of the end for Arthur. The two lovers fled to Lancelot's land in Brittany, France. Arthur decided to follow and wage war on his former friend, leaving his nephew Mordred as custodian of England. Whilst he was battling across the English Channel, Mordred rebelled, so Arthur was forced to return home. A fierce battle ensued on Salisbury Plain. Arthur managed to kill Mordred, but the king himself was also mortally wounded. On the brink of death, he returned to Avalon. He is said to have thrown Excalibur into the kingdom's lake and then he himself disappeared into a cave, saying he would return when England was in great danger.

The first historical proof we have of a Arthurian-type figure is in Gildas' sixth century De Excidio Britanniae which refers to British soldiers being led by a man called Ambrosius Aurelianus. The name 'Arthur' appears in Nennius' ninth century Historia Brittonium. However it was not until the twelfth century that the phenomenon of Arthur as an historical icon really had an impact. William of Malmesbury and Geoffrey of Monmouth produced works which sowed the seeds of our modern understanding of Athurian legend. Unfortunately their works also included many fictional details, which have subsequently obscured the true reality of Arthur's reign.

There is other evidence for his place in historical fact. Many people believe that Glastonbury in Somerset is the true site of Camelot, and in the 12th century it was claimed that Arthur's grave had been found there. Similarly, the Isles of Scilly are said to host the remains of the great king. Certainly there are plenty of candidates for places featured in Arthurian mythology and historians have discovered many possible historical figures who could be the king himself. The historians believe that the sheer

number of possibilities as to Arthur's true identity is probably the reason that our knowledge has become so blurred, and that many individual personal histories have been actually confused and amalgamated.

What we do know is that in the sixth century many Celtic realms had leaders born who were called Arthur; this could have been in homage to the original king. Although the use of the name has clouded the original Arthur's legend, it also points to the fact that a truly great and inspirational leader was present a generation before.

Perhaps that most amazing evidence has only surfaced in recent years. In July 1998, archaeologists found a slab marked in Latin with the name 'Artagnov' or 'Arthnou' on a rocky hilltop in Tintagel, Cornwall. The slab dates to the sixth century, and proves that the name was present in the legendary Arthurian lands at the correct time, and belonged to a man of some standing. Like many historical mysteries, the damage to truth caused by passing years, is slowly being fixed by science and the application of modern interest. We may never know exactly who the legend of King Arthur represents, but with more finds like this, we can only move closer to the tantalising truth.

MAITREYA

ALL THE WORLD'S major religions expect another visit by a supremely holy man. Hindus await the arrival of Krishna; Jews expect the appearance of a Messiah; Muslims believe in an Imam Mahdi; Christians expect the Second Coming of Christ and Buddhists imagine Him as a Buddha. There is a large organisation operating across the world which believes

these various figures all refer to the same, single being, that He is a teacher sent to direct Mankind towards a future of peace and love, and that this being already walks amongst us – in fact, he lives in a suburb of London.

The Share International Magazine company operates as the mouthpiece for this great leader whom they call Maitreya. The organisation's leading light is Benjamin Creme, a former artist from Glasgow born in 1922. Creme is a follower of Theosophy, the movement created by Madame Helena Blavatsky, whose members believe that Earth and Humanity is controlled by a select council of inter-dimensional super-beings.

Creme believes these super-beings or 'Masters' told him in 1975 of Maitreya's impending appearance, and gave him the task of preparing for his arrival. Many people think that Creme sees himself as a modern day John the Baptist, and uses Share International to promote the Maitreya cause. He writes books and articles and appears on television shows and in lecture halls discussing the upcoming Maitreya unveiling.

Creme says Maitreya emerged from a spiritual centre in the Himalayas on 19th July 1977, and flew to Europe by aeroplane. He then disappeared into an ethnic community in a suburb of London, and has lived quite anonymously ever since. However, the Tara Centre, another organisation close to Creme, has run a series of full-page adverts in major newspapers across the world announcing the presence of the 'Lord Maitreya.' It is even said that a major American television network has asked to interview Maitreya at any time of his choosing.

Maitreya has also made some personal appearances. One of the most celebrated happened on 11th June 1988 in Nairobi, when 6000 worshippers in the village of Kawangware saw him appear in the form of Jesus Christ. The white-robed, bearded figure walked among them and declared that the world was 'nearing the time for the reign of heaven.' Maitreya then left in a car. Share International also claims that Maitreya has performed many miracles. The phenomenon is spreading throughout Africa, and many villages are being visited by the man in white.

In 1996 there was the biggest outbreak of strange 'crosses of light' reports in recent years. CBS television news broadcast a story about 40-feet-high glowing crosses which had appeared in the windows of a Baptist Church in Knoxville, Tennessee. The local priest said 30,000 people came to view the bizarre sight and miraculous happenings have since occurred there. Similar crosses of light have appeared throughout the world, and Share International claims this is a sign of Maitreya being in our world.

Share International claims that before his public appearances, Maitreya likes to energise local water sources. Magic water in the little town of Tlacote in Mexico is said to heal everything from AIDS and cancer to obesity and high cholesterol. Other miraculous water is said to have sprung up at a disused slate mine at Nordenau, 100km east of Dusseldorf in Germany. In August 1994 a strange image of the Madonna and Child appeared on a church wall in the small South Australia town of Yankalilla. A dowser came to the site and said there was water running underneath the church. Benjamin Creme informed them that this was the work of Maitreya and said the water would have healing powers. Creme told the Yankalilla people where to dig, and sure enough, a miraculous spring was discovered.

Share International has performed some miracles of its own. It is now an official non-governmental organisation recognised by the United Nations, and has published articles written by some very respected figures – Boutros Boutros-Ghali, Kofi Annan, Mary Robinson, the Dalai Lama and Prince Charles amongst others. The future of Maitreya is uncertain depending on your belief. If you are a follower, his appearances will only increase until he becomes a global voice. If not, he will quietly disappear just as the dozens of self-proclaiming Messiahs over the centuries always have.

THE MAN IN THE IRON MASK

OF ALL THE MYSTERIOUS figures in history, no one has sparked more interest, and provided such little detail, as the Man in the Iron Mask. Despite more than 300 years of puzzle, conjecture and uncertainty, there are precious few clues to his identity. The man is a enigmatic character who has been the subject of a classic novel by Alexandre Dumas and countless feature films. His place in the public's mind is assured, but despite arousing such popular interest, no crucial revelations have been discovered. All we know is that he was a distinguished prisoner, and from the moment he was imprisoned, he had to hide his identity behind a strange mask.

The Man in the Iron Mask was first imprisoned sometime in the 1660s, probably towards the end of the decade. He was initially jailed at the fortress of Pignerol in the French Alps, where he was guarded by Benigne d'Auvergne de Saint-Mars, who would continue to be his personal jailer until the mysterious man's death. He was transferred to the nearby prison in Exiles in 1681, and then to the island castle of Sainte Marguerite in 1687. It was during this second change of jail that the first witness account reported seeing a prisoner in an iron mask. In 1698 Saint-Mars was made the governor of the Bastille, the famous Parisian prison. Consequently, the masked man moved to the French capital and more reports, this time of a man in a black velvet mask, were recorded. He is said to have died in the Bastille in 1703.

The actual details we have of his life are extremely scant. A death certificate states the prisoner's name was Marchioly, and he was about 45 years old when he died. This seems unlikely, particularly as he had been held in captivity for almost 40 years. One man who initiated many theories about the Bastille's mysterious inmate was another, later, resident of the jail – the philosopher and writer Voltaire who had spoken to the man's captors. He revealed that the man had been in jail since 1661, and was young, tall and handsome when first captured. He was said to dress in exquisite clothing, had refined hobbies and tastes and, crucially, he looked very much like a member of the French Royal Family.

Although Voltaire was a known adversary of French Royalty, this suggestion that the prisoner was possibly a twin brother of King Louis XIV lingered, and was adopted by Dumas for his novel. Despite the fact that an identical physical resemblance to the king would account for the man being permanently masked, it seems unlikely that such a monumental fact could have stayed a secret.. However, the king's birth did have some unusual qualities, and there is a strong possibility that the prisoner may have been an illegitimate brother of Louis XIV.

Other theories for the masked man's identity include that he was actually the playwright Moliére, who had been imprisoned for fear of corrupting the king. This can be discounted because Moliére would have been too old to fit the dates recorded. There are also suggestions that he

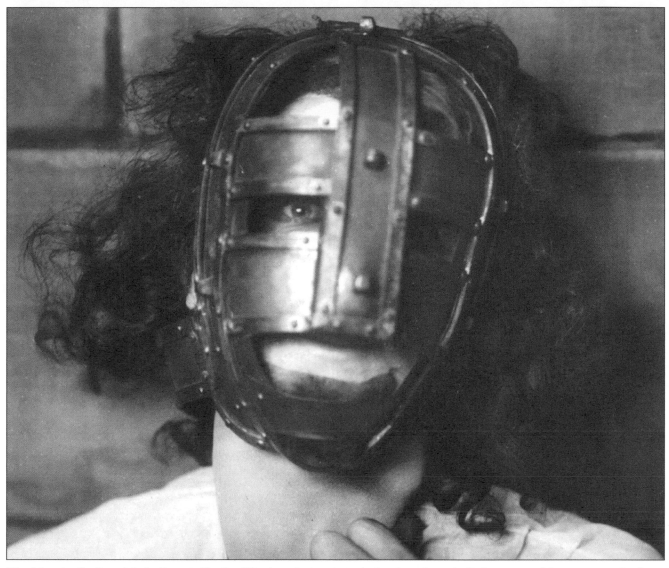

The Man in the Iron Mask. Reputedly the King's unfortunate twin brother, there is little or no evidence as to whether he ever existed or not.

may have been Nicolas Fouquet, a envied wealthy French nobleman, or even an illegitimate lovechild of Charles II of England.

What cannot be in doubt is the reverence with which he was treated. Saint-Mars was known to call him, 'my prince,' and his guarding soldiers referred to him as 'Tower.' It has even been revealed that the soldiers would often remove their hats when entering his chamber, and would stand silently until the man motioned them to sit. In 1711, Princess Palatine, the king's sister-in-law, wrote a letter about how the man was flanked at all times by two musketeers who had orders to immediately kill him if he

removed his mask. Similarly, letters between the king and Saint-Mars have revealed that the prisoner should be executed straight away if he tried to talk or communicate with anybody.

Certainly, the prisoner warranted special attention, whoever he was. Many experts have wondered why, if he was such a threat to the French Royal Family, he was not just executed anyway. However, the fact that was allowed to live, but only behind a mask, perhaps does indicate he had an interesting relationship with the monarchy. The identity of the Man in the Iron Mask is now a fact lost in time, and the true story of his life is probably a tale we will never fully know.

NOSTRADAMUS

IN THE MODERN AGE, Michel de Nostradamus is associated with one simple notion – prophecies of doom. This has been derived from his great work The Centuries, a collection of around 1,000 four-line verses or quatrains. Nostradamus believed that through his study of astrology, combined with divine guidance, he was able to see the future. He used meditation, mild hallucinogens and extreme focus to heighten his images. The first part of The Centuries was published in 1555 – the verses contained a strange and vague language, which Nostradamus claimed he had used purposefully to refute charges of witchcraft. Written in a mixture of French with occasional inclusions of Latin, Greek and Italian, many people now believe they can decipher these verses, and Nostradamus has been hailed as an accurate foreteller of things to come. However, these enthusiasts have had the privilege of hindsight and the luxury of fitting real events to suit his text. Few of predictions made at the end of the 20th century about the start of the new millennium, which cited his work as reference, have come to pass. So how good a seer was Nostradamus?

Probably the most famous example of Nostradamus' work is that which many enthusiasts say predicted the Second World War. The text itself, taken from Century 2, Quatrain 24, in translation reads:

Beasts ferocious from hunger will swim across rivers:

The greater part of the region will be against the Hister,

Michel de Nostradamus, perhaps the world's most famous seer.

The great one will cause it to be dragged in an iron cage,

When the Germany child will observes nothing.

Nostradamus believers suggest 'Hister' is Hitler; the 'ferocious beasts' are invading Nazis 'hungry' for power; but the German nation, who blindly follow, without fully realising or grasping events, will be imprisoned. There is a ring of truth about that interpretation. But sceptics point out that there are no dates involved; terms like 'ferocious beasts,' and 'the great one' are particularly ambiguous and imprecise, and the Hister is actually a region near the River Danube, not Hitler. However, other quatrains nearby in the text do seem to mention other important details about the war, and Hitler's personal history shows that he was born near the Danube. So perhaps, taken as a whole, there is something there.

In recent years, the new millennium and World Trade Centre attack have caused a major re-examination and interest in Nostradamus' work. Perhaps the most memorable figure mentioned in verses said to relate to our own time is that of 'Mabus' or 'Maddas.' This person is said to be – if I can be similarly non-committal – the next 'great evil.' In the 1990s, many Nostradamus readers claimed he was definitely called 'Maddas,' which just happens to be 'Saddam' spelt backwards, so it was clear where their finger was pointing. However, after 11th September 2001, the spelling became something closer to Mabus which is an anagram of Usam B. As I write this, enthusiasts interpreting his works are in something of a state of flux, and are not quite sure which Middle Eastern villain is the one predicted.

After the World Trade Centre attack, a great flood of false Nostradamus verses appeared throughout the information networks. This confused many people, and increased scepticism about his work among the not-so–credulous. That is something of a shame, particularly as there are good arguments to suggest he predicted the death of John F. Kennedy, the fall of Communism, the French Revolution and the Challenger Space Shuttle disaster. But the unconvinced will always refer to the vague language, absence of definite dates, and benefit of back cataloguing events as areas of doubt. If anybody is interested, he predicts the end of the world in 3797.

Certainly, people of his own period believed in his powers, medical and otherwise. The Queen of France, Catherine de Medici asked him to plot the horoscope of

At work in his study, Nostradamus stops to ponder the meaning of it all.

her husband King Henry II, and in 1564 he was appointed court physician to King Charles IX of France. His final prediction came true on 2nd July 1556. The day before, as he left a meeting with his priest, the clergyman is believed to have said 'Until tomorrow,' to which Nostradamus replied, 'You will not find me alive at sunrise.' Sure enough, by the morning he was dead. It is said that his body is buried with a script which translates his prophecies into more defined predictions. Perhaps this could finally put to rest the debate about just how good a foreseer Nostradamus really was.

Queen of Sheba

THE MYSTICAL FIGURE known as the Queen of Sheba is recorded in the First Book of Kings in the Old Testament. It states that around the tenth century BC a queen of the rich trading nation, known as Sheba decided to meet the great King Solomon in person. She did not believe the stories she had been told of Solomon's wisdom, and brought many hard questions to test him. When his replies met with her approval she gave him plentiful gifts of gold, spices and precious stones. In return, Solomon gave the queen 'all her desire,' and after their meeting she returned to her own country. The story is repeated in the second Book of Chronicles, and even Christ himself spoke of a queen of the south who came to hear the wisdom of Solomon. Other than this, precious few pieces of historical evidence have survived, but that has not stopped the growth of countless myths and stories. So who was the real Queen of Sheba?

Perhaps the most famous and important extension of her story is that connected with Ethiopia. In 1320 an Ethiopian monk named Yetshak wrote a compendium of legends called 'Kebra Negast' or 'Glory of the Kings.' In it, he said that when the Queen of Sheba, referred to in Ethiopian as Makeda, visited Solomon, she was seduced by the great king. Solomon had said that the queen was welcome to his hospitality, but must not take anything without asking. During the night, the Queen suffered a terrible thirst caused by a spicy meal Solomon fed her and she drank the water placed by her bed. The king said she had broken the rules, and must sleep with him as repayment. Nine months later

The Queen of Sheba.

she gave birth to a boy called Menelik. Ethiopians believe that the Queen and her son both accepted the Jewish faith, and that Menelik founded the Solomon Jewish, and then Christian, dynasty in Aksum, Ethiopia.

At around the same time as Yetshak was compiling his tome, other legends were forming in Europe. A thirteenth century

Who was the real Queen of Sheba?

story told in the Legenda Aurea stated that the queen was a prophetess connected to the crucifixion of Christ. Over time, she also became an integral part of religious decorations and art. She was often seen as a sorceress, and then a seductress. Strangely, she is also featured as having a secret deformity – French Gothic sculpture often shows her having a webbed foot. In the same way, Gustave Flaubert's Temptation of Saint Anthony depicts the queen as a lustful temptress with a withered limb.

This imperfection perhaps arises from earlier Jewish and Islamic references to her. In both the Koran and the Jewish Book called the Targum Sheni, the queen meets Solomon and reveals that she has hairy feet. The Jewish tradition later features her as a demon or seductress, whereas Islamic legend states that Solomon used his magicians' power to remove her excess hair and married her. Muslims call the Queen of Sheba Balkis, and believe her great nation was based in the Yemen. The Koran describes Sheba as being two gardens, irrigated by a great dam. An advanced level of farming, and good access to Red Sea shipping channels and Arabian camel trains, meant the nation prospered.

Archaeological proof of this occurring in Southern Arabia has been uncovered. The remains of a great dam can be viewed in the Mareb region of the Yemen, now considered to be the capital of the ancient Sheba nation. This dam collapsed in AD543, but scientists have been able to deduce that it would have been used to irrigate over 500 acres of farm land. In recent years, archaeologists have finished restoring an ancient temple known as the 'Throne of Balkis' in the Mareb region. The structure dates from the tenth century BC, so is from the right era to link with what we do know about the queen. Two miles to the east of the Marab region, another ancient building, known as the 'Temple of the Moon God,' is also being studied. Scientists using radar equipment believe this is an extremely large and elaborate structure, and could yield the answers to many Sheba mysteries. Unfortunately such investigations have been plagued over the years by political indifference and, until these areas become more secure for researchers to study, the true history of Sheba may continue to be obscured by myth and legend.

URI GELLER

URI GELLER IS, without doubt, the most famous proponent of psychic powers in the world today. Unlike past figures who have claimed mysterious talents, Geller has had to prove his abilities in front of an ever-developing media and an increasingly intelligent public. Many sceptics, however, are dubious of his claims and believe he is nothing more than a simple illusionist. Having said that, popular culture across the world continues to view Geller with a degree of respect and awe and even scientists are beginning to question if he has tapped into an unexplained natural power. So is Uri Geller a phenomenon or a faker?

The world at large first encountered Uri Geller in the 1970s, when the young Israeli arrived in Europe. Born on 20th December 1946 to Hungarian and Austrian parents, Geller had already became something of a celebrity in his homeland for displaying unusual abilities. He had performed amazing feats of telepathy and psychokinesis to small audiences across the country, which had fascinated the Israeli population. Geller claims he had only developed these powers after an encounter with a ball of light at the age of four and that during his childhood he discovered the ability to bend cutlery with minimal contact. However, it was not until he had completed a term of service in the Israeli army, and then worked as a model that he decided to exhibit his powers.

In 1972 Geller left Israel and an appearance on the Talk-In television show in Britain turned him into an instant celebrity. He performed other demonstrations across Europe and, using only mind power,

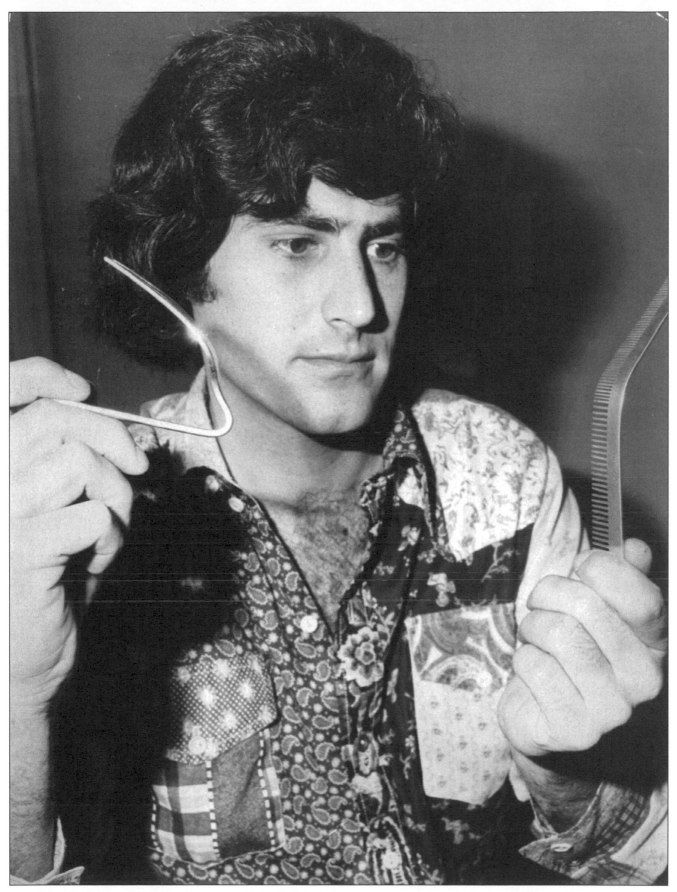

Uri Geller demonstrates his amazing metal-bending skills for the cameras. Whether or not Geller possesses the pyschic skills he claims for himself, his ability with metal seems beyond doubt.

managed to stop a cable car and an escalator from working in Germany. His celebrity grew quickly and widely, and he was asked to visit the United States to exhibit his abilities there. Many of the American scientific community were eager to view the human phenomenon, and Geller was subjected to all manner of tests at many of the country's leading institutions. One of the eminent men he met was Dr Wernher von Braun, the leading mind behind NASA's rocket programme, and the man widely dubbed the 'Father of the Space Age.' Von Braun was one of the first to experience Geller effects up close when the young visitor managed to bend the older scientist's wedding ring without any physical contact.

Under laboratory conditions at the Stanford Research Institute, Geller was able to prove high levels of predictive talents and managed to alter weight measurements using only mind control. At London's Birkbeck College he evoked extreme Geiger counter readings and manipulated crystal formations psychically. One of his most impressive performances was at the high security US Navy Weapons base at Silver Springs in Maryland. Here, Geller used his mind control talents to fundamentally alter the structure of a newly-created metal called Nitinol. Despite this, he is most well known for spoon bending and clock stopping, and Geller claims he was the cause of Big Ben's three breakdowns in the 1990s.

Indeed, Geller's relevance to the scientific community has been superseded by his celebrity status. He has featured on the front cover of most major international magazines and papers. He has appeared on television and radio shows across the world, and there has even been a film called 'Mindbender' produced which depicts his life. Over 15 books have been written about him, and he has featured in countless more. In all, he is now something of a world-wide celebrity.

Geller himself seems to have embraced his famous status, and considers people like Michael Jackson and David Blaine among his close friends. He has had cameo roles in numerous movies and programmes and was one of the original contestants in the British version of the reality TV programme I'm A Celebrity – Get Me Out Of Here. He has also branched out to produce art and pottery, and has even recorded a selection of songs. In recent years his business interests have developed in the technological inventions market and he has created equipment which can differentiate between real and fake banknotes and diamonds.

All this may enhance the image, popularity and celebrity of Uri Geller, but it does nothing to promote serious study of his powers. That is a shame because many eminent experts seem to believe he has abilities far beyond the realm of most modern-day men.

SECRET SOCIETIES AND HIDDEN TREASURES

Knights Templars

A GROUP OF NINE French knights founded an order in Jerusalem in 1118 under the title 'The Poor Knights of Christ.' The warriors all took monastic views and pledged their lives to protecting Christian travellers and the Holy Land. They were housed at the palace of King Baldwin II, the French King of Jerusalem, on the site of Solomon's Temple which is how they gained their title 'Knights Templar.' In 1128 they were officially sanctioned by Pope Honorius II, and they were provided with a 'Rule' from Saint Bernard of Clairvaux. The knights gained a fearsome reputation for being ferocious in battle, courageous and honourable. They fought in the Crusades alongside Richard the Lionheart and quickly accumulated vast amounts of treasure, wealth and land from grateful European monarchs.

Within 200 years the Templars had left the Holy Land and taken residence in Paris, but such was their influence that they were only required to answer to the Pope. Their riches were so immense that they began the earliest form of organised banking, and became known as moneylenders to European monarchies. But this, combined with a history of holding meetings in secret, led to their downfall. King Philip the Fair of France was known to be hugely indebted with staggering sums owed to the order. On 13th October 1307, he declared that the Templars engaged in heretical activities at their meetings, arrested all members of the order in France, and seized their assets. The Templars accepted his decisions quietly, but many were then tortured into giving false confessions of unholy practises. However, only the Pope could condemn the order, and a newly installed Pope Clement V was happy to bow to Philip's coercions.

The order was disbanded, and it was suggested that all European monarchies take steps to suppress the movement. On 19th March 1314, the last Grand Master of the Knights Templar, Jacques de Molay, was burned at the stake on an island in the middle of the River Seine in Paris. As the flames rose, it is claimed de Molay cursed King Philip and Pope threatening that they would both follow him within a year. They both did – Clement died a month later and Philip seven months after that. However, the Knights Templar themselves are said to have continued in secret, and before his death, de Molay had passed on his powers to a successor. Some of the Templars are believed to have taken refuge in Scotland during the intervening years, but the movement did not reveal itself again until 1705.

Since then the order has had associations with Freemasonry and other secret societies, but the movement has flourished and they have had many high profile and influential members. In more recent years, following the Second World War, the cohesion of the entire international order has become somewhat fractured. The meetings are still held in secret.

Apart from fiercely guarded rituals ands traditions, it would seem that there are few

The Knights Templar. Did they hide a huge treasure away from the grasping King Philip of France?

Jacques de Molay, leader of the Templars.

from their buildings. Philip never found all the riches in their offices that he wished to acquire, and it seems the knights submitted to his thuggery meekly, in order to let their great treasure escape. So what was this treasure? The obvious theory is that it was gold and jewels taken from holy temples of Jerusalem and the biblical world during the Crusades. However, many have speculated that the reaction of the Templars suggested that it was something beyond material value, and may have been something of enormous spiritual importance, such as the Ark of the Covenant or the Holy Grail. Others have considered that it may be secret Christian knowledge, such as the 'bloodline of Jesus Christ.'

The treasure, whatever nature it takes, has never been found, and where it is hidden remains a mystery. Many Templar experts have considered it may have been the root of Bérenger Saunière's mysterious wealth, and believe it was buried at the church of Rennes-le-Château. However, one of the most widely-held theories is that the surviving Templars hid it at Rosslyn Chapel in Scotland. If the order did manage to continue throughout its banished years, there is good reason to believe the secrets of the treasure are known to only a select few. To the rest of us, the Knights Templar are only modern day descendants of an historical mystery.

mysteries surrounding the order. But one question remains – why did the Parisian Templars not fight when arrested by Philip's men? In the days leading to their capture, a heavily-laden cart was supposedly removed

RENNES-LE-CHÂTEAU

THE LEGEND OF Rennes-le-Château is one of the most complicated treasure-hunting stories of all time. It is steeped in the movements of pre-medieval European dynasties and encompasses a whole host of historical unsolved mysteries. Enthusiasts believe the secret of Rennes-le-Château could reveal the whereabouts of the Holy Grail, or the Ark of the Covenant, or indeed almost any other lost treasure. The story involves mysterious societies like the Knights Templar, the Freemasons and the Priory of the Sion. Researchers say that many of those who have been told any of the real details have died in suspicious circumstances. Their fate, and the village's enigmatic story, all revolved around the arrival of one man.

On 1st June 1885, a recently ordained priest entered the hot, dusty, hilltop village of Rennes-le-Château in the French Pyrenees. Bérenger Saunière was an ambitious young cleric, and was very unimpressed by the dilapidated ninth century church and the uninhabitable presbytery, although he stayed. In October of that year Saunière was banished from the region for a short time for committing a public order offence when he campaigned against the ruling Republican Party. During this exile from his parish he formed a friendship with the wealthy and respected Countess of Chambord, who loaned him a large sum to rebuild the village church. He began the restoration work five years later, starting with the altar. As he removed the heavy stone lintel, the ancient pillar on which it stood cracked, and inside it Saunière found three wooden tubes containing parchments. After finding another scrap of paper in a pillar supporting the pulpit, Saunière immediately began digging up parts of the church and its yard.

Helped in this by his housekeeper, Marie Denarnaud, Saunière recorded in his personal diary on 21st September 1891, 'Excavated a grave. Found a tomb.' What was found in the tomb is unknown, but over the following years Saunière led a very odd life. He built an elaborate estate, which had gardens full of exotic flora and fauna. The whole structure was said to be a recreation of Mary Magdalene's walk from Magdala to Bethania. Saunière lived in splendour and was said to hold accounts in various major banks. He was known to visit Paris and mix with famous people, but regional church authorities grew tired of his strange behaviour and tried to discipline him. Saunière said he needed to answer to nobody but the Pontiff and resigned his seat. The villagers of Rennes-le-Château chose to attend Mass at Saunière's private chapel rather than attend the one provided by the officially installed new priest.

On 17th January 1917 Saunière had a serious seizure, and shortly before his death explained how he had come to find his wealth. The priest who heard the details was so disgusted he denied Saunière absolution and last rites. But Denarnaud also knew the secret and promised to reveal it on her deathbed. Unfortunately she suffered a debilitating stroke and could not talk when she died in 1953. Others who may have understood some aspects of the mysteries suffered horrific fates. Many people believe Denarnaud's carer, Noel Corbu, may have learnt something from her before her death, but he was killed in a car accident in the same year. Another local priest, Jean-Antoine-Maurice Gelis, was said to know details during Saunière's time, but he grew so paranoid that he would let only his niece into his presbytery. On All Saints' Eve 1897, he was found killed by four blows from an axe. During an investigation in 1956 the corpses of three men who had been shot were found in Saunière's garden, and in 1967 Fakhur el Islam, a courier carrying Saunière's secret documents, was found dead on train tracks near Melun in Germany.

It is believed that a secretive society called the Priory of Sion is behind much of the strange history of Rennes-le-Château. The group is said to have strong connections with Freemasons and legends of the Holy Grail. It has been a registered organisation in France since 1956 and has over a thousand members, some of whom are extremely high profile. The Grand Master until 1963 was Jean Cocteau, and past leaders have included Claude Debussy, Leonardo de Vinci and Isaac Newton. Yet, despite this air of respectability, the organisation is still said to be untraceable. Saunière himself was not so secretive about the treasure though, and it is believed he left many clues in the buildings he erected and the monuments he left. The design of the church in Rennes-le-Château itself is supposed to be a clue about the treasure. One theory is that Saunière's wealth came about by his discovery of details relating to an old Christian secret, which he then used to blackmail the Roman Catholic Church.

One of the stained glass windows he had commissioned after rebuilding the church

Statue of a demon, most likely of Lucifer.

depicts both Mary and Joseph holding babies, which has lead some to suspect Saunière had proof that Christ had a twin. Similarly, it has been considered that perhaps the priest found evidence that Jesus did not die on the cross, but moved to Europe and had a family with Mary Magdalene. Many of the blackmail ideas seem to revolve around elaborate conspiracy theories, but there are also legends of real, sparkling, mystical treasure. Rennes-le-Château is believed to have been the third largest town in the Visigoth kingdom, when it was known as Rheddae. Visgoths were said to have looted Rome of all its riches in 410 AD and were also believed to have stolen great wealth from Greece and Jerusalem. It was never disclosed exactly where the Visigoths finally buried their treasure, although the fortress of Rheddae was always considered a strong possibility.

Another theory combines aspects of both treasure and religious secrecy. It is suggested that the Cathars, a Christian group who were considered a threat by the Roman Catholic Church, buried something of immense religious importance near Rennes-le-Château before they were destroyed. Some have suggested that this great spiritual treasure may have been the Holy Grail or Ark of the Covenant. The great French classical artist, Nicolas Poussin, is also said to have known of the secrets of Rennes-le-Château. He apparently included clues in a number of his paintings; particularly one called Les Bergers d'Arcadie which features a tomb that closely resembles one found near to Rennes-le-Château.

Many factors pointing to the truth behind Saunière's wealth are still available for study. But despite the best efforts of countless experts, these mysteries remain hidden. Did Saunière find a legendary religious artefact, a horde of ancient treasure, or some terrible Christian secret? The answers may, one day, be revealed, but for now, Saunière and his money continue to be a curious puzzle.

THE ARK OF THE COVENANT

THE BIBLE SAYS that God inscribed the Ten Commandments on two stone tablets that he gave to Moses. To protect the tablets, and to let them be carried, a wooden chest decorated with exquisite gold ornaments was built. It was about three-and-a-half feet long, just over two feet wide, and had two poles attached through gold rings on its sides. There were two carved cherubim on top, and the chest's lid was called the atonement cover or the 'mercy seat.' The box accompanied Moses and the Israelites on their quest for the Promised Land, and brought them victory wherever they went. When they finally founded Jerusalem, King Solomon built the 'Holy of Holies,' or First Temple, and housed the box there. This supremely holy chest is called the Ark of the Covenant.

No single item is involved in more legends of treasure, unexplained wealth and international intrigue than this great chest. Some legends say that the Ark was destroyed or captured by invading Egyptian forces around 925BC, others say that the Babylonians stole it in 586BC. The Jewish sect who wrote the Dead Sea Scrolls may have buried the Ark in the Jordanian desert before they were overrun. Likewise, it has been suggested that an early Christian group called the Cathars may have hidden it in an ancient church at Rennes-le-Château in France before they were destroyed by the Catholic Church.

King Arthur has also been linked to the

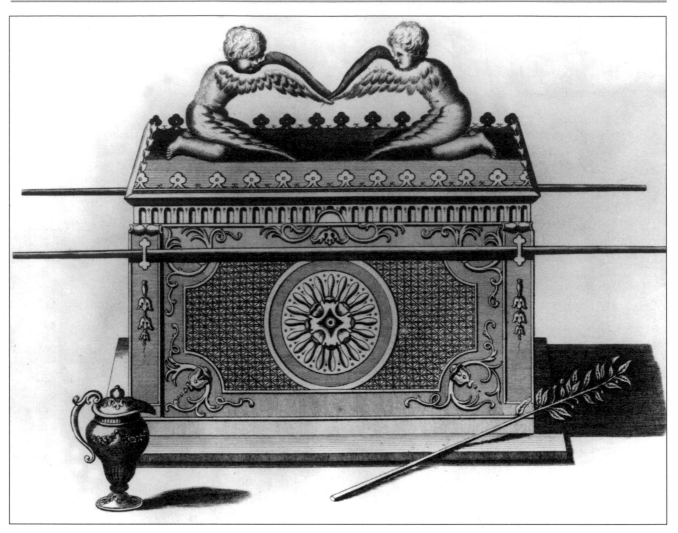

Fanciful impression of the Ark of the Covenant, reputed to contain the original Ten Commandments.

Ark's history, whilst many researchers claim it was taken from the Holy Land by the Knights Templar. It is said that they may have hidden it at the pit on Oak Island, or even at a Scottish chapel in Rosslyn. Conspiracy theorists believe the descendants of the Knights Templar are the Freemasons, who now have the Ark under their control. In fact, many mysterious tales have incorporated aspects of involving the Ark of the Covenant. Here, we will look at two of the most plausible theories.

Leen Ritmeyer is an archaeologist who has conducted tests on Temple Mount in Jerusalem, and believes he has established the true position of the First Temple. He claims he has discovered a section cut out of the underlying rock that exactly matches the dimensions of the Ark. From this, Ritmeyer believes the Ark may be buried deep inside Temple Mount, but it seems impossible that excavations will be carried out in the area, particularly whilst it continues to be the site of violent political turmoil. Many other experts also believe the Ark remains in the Holy Land, and one, an American called Ron Wyatt, even claimed to have found the sacred chest in the Garden Tomb, in the north of the old city of Jerusalem.

Perhaps the most celebrated theory connecting the Ark with a real object revolves around western Africa. Ethiopia has a legend that claims the Queen of Sheba was impregnated by King Solomon. The child, known as Menelik, meaning 'the son of the wiseman,' travelled to Jerusalem when he was 20 to study in his father's court. Within a year, Solomon's priests had become jealous of the king's son and said he must return to Sheba. Solomon accepted this but said that all first-born sons of other elders should accompany Menelik. One of these, Azarius, was the son of Zadok, the High Priest. It was Azarius who stole the Ark and took it to Africa. Menelik decided that their success must be divine will, and founded the 'Second Jerusalem' at Aksum in Ethiopia. Today, the ancient church of St Mary of Zion is said to house the Ark, which was traditionally brought out every January for the celebration known as Timkat.

In recent years, due to the instability in the country, the Ark has been hidden away and cared for by a devoted guardian, who is the only man allowed to see the true nature of the box. Certainly, there is a lot to recommend this theory – for instance, Ethiopians are one of the few races that practise Christianity in Africa, and the national constitution ruled that the Ethiopian emperor is a direct descendant of Solomon. Ethiopians are confident of their role in the Arks heritage, but with so many legends vying to reveal the final resting place of the Ark of the Covenant, it is impossible to decide on one. Perhaps, as many religious groups believe, its presence will become known when the time is right.

THE HOLY GRAIL

ALMOST ALL OF our understanding of the Holy Grail is derived from romantic Arthurian tales of the twelfth and thirteenth centuries. However, there are some generally accepted details. The Grail is believed to be the chalice of the Eucharist or dish of the Pascal lamb used by Christ at the Last Supper. This vessel was taken by Joseph of Arimathea, who used it to collect blood from the crucified body of Christ. An alternative theory is that it was a chalice given to Joseph by Christ in a vision This vessel's holy powers sustained Joseph for 42 years during his incarceration by the Jews. In either case, Joseph brought the holy chalice to Britain, thus beginning the true legend.

Some people believe the Holy Grail was secretly passed down through generations of Joseph's descendants. Others believe it is buried in the Chalice Well at Britain's oldest holy city, Glastonbury, which indicates a connection to Arthurian legend. Romantic tales say that Arthur and his Knights of the Round Table set off on a holy quest to find the Grail. More reliable legend says the Cathars had possession of the Grail and hid it in the Pyrenees before they were over-run.

It has been suggested that they may have kept it at their stronghold of Montségur, which was actually searched by Nazi forces looking for the Grail during the Second World War. Others believe the Cathars hid it at Rennes-le-Château, or gave the chalice to the Knights Templar for safe-keeping. Some researchers believe a field in Shropshire hides the Grail under its surface, and another tradition states that a wooden cup in a Welsh country house is the true artefact. The organised church does not credit any legend

Our understanding of the Holy Grail is derived from romantic Arthurian tales of the twelfth and thirteenth centuries

of its existence, although that should not be seen as any indication that it is purely a myth. Whether any evidence of the fabled chalice's existence is ever found or not, the story of the Holy Grail will continue to puzzle Man for many years to come.

184

ALCHEMY

THE DISCOVERY OF OXYGEN in the eighteenth century is largely believed to have led to the birth of chemistry as we know it. Before then, many races had examined the properties of different materials without ever forming a coherent theory to link their qualities; these ancient studies were known as alchemy or transmutation. Scientists had believed that as metals oxidised, so they gained an important addition. They thought the ultimate transmutation process would turn substances into gold or silver. Today, alchemy is largely considered to be this idea of creating gold. Modern chemistry has proven such a theory is completely impossible, but for thousands of years it was not always thought to be so.

Certainly, many of the greatest minds the world has ever seen believed in the possibility of making gold from base ingredients. In fact, it was such a widely held belief that King Henry IV of England actually encouraged all intelligent men in the country to study the subject so that the nation's great debts could be paid. Similarly, in later years, many rulers supported alchemists and their experiments. Other races feared the repercussions of transmutation success, and in the second century BC China actually made the production of gold by alchemy an offence punishable by death. The Roman Emperor Diocletian even ordered the destruction of all Egyptian texts that advocated alchemical procedures.

Diocletian and the Chinese authorities were wise to be wary, for the Ancient Egyptian and Oriental peoples were known to be the masters of alchemy. Mystical Eastern practices are still revered by some to this day, and the Egyptians are said to have spread their knowledge onto other races. The Arabic world was one of the recipients, and the seventh century King Khalid was said to be a master of the subject. Indeed, the word 'alchemy' is thought to have been derived from the Arabic for Egyptian art, 'al-khem.' In the following centuries it is said that the Sufi Islamic movement used alchemy as part of their religious beliefs.

Certainly, alchemy has always had strong religious connections. Albertus Magnus and St. Thomas Aquinas were both experts on the subject. Aquinas even wrote a text asking if it was ethically correct to pass off gold created by alchemy as real gold. Another holy man, the fourteenth century Pope John XXII, is credited with writing a major work on the subject, and also wrote a great text damning fraudulent alchemists. When he died in 1334, he left the Church 18 million florins of gold bullion, which no one had even realised he had acquired. Even Martin Luther is believed to have said alchemy was beneficial for affirming church doctrines, whilst the grandees of modern science, Boyle and Newton, were also sympathetic to alchemy.

Although modern chemistry has revealed that what the alchemists were aiming for is impossible, even today our knowledge grows in strange ways. The realm of unstable radioactive materials and the notion that the physical construction of subjects can be

Alchemists at work. The idea of changing base metals into gold has had an enduring fascination down the ages.

altered has opened new avenues of thought. Similarly, another goal of alchemy was to find the elixir of life that would cure all ills and make men young for eternity. Again, although modern science has dismissed alchemist's methods, experiments in the fields of DNA and cloning have suggested that it is a notion not too far removed from reality. It was even an alchemist, Paracelsus who, in the sixteenth century, determined that illnesses were caused by foreign agents attacking the body.

Other off-shoots of this medical branch of alchemy are also held as valid in our modern age. Homeopathy and aromatherapy are direct descendants of old alchemy studies, and acupuncture and hypnosis are also connected. Some modern alchemists still believe however that illness is caused by an imbalance in the body, so much of the medical profession regard them as 'quacks.' Similarly, the subject has been linked with many New Age ideas and theories which has not helped the public accept it as a genuine and serious area of interest. Many people continue to practise alchemy and maintain that it is a valid subject. Science tends to disagree, but our development and view of the world still owes a lot to this ancient art.

THE ROSICRUCIANS

IN 1614, A PAMPHLET called Fama Fraternitatis Rosae Crucis, was published. It described a secret brotherly order of non-Catholic Christians who were striving for knowledge of alchemy and magic. This group, known as the 'Rosicrucian Brotherhood,' was said to be founded in 1408 by a former monk and nobleman Christian Rosenkreuz. Rosenkreuz was thought to have travelled through Damascus, Jerusalem and Fez, and had acquired knowledge of magical Arabian learnings and Egyptian spiritualism. The Rosicrucian movement he inspired was believed capable of making gold, and was devoted to the secret study of nature's mystical properties. They were said to be concerned with encouraging the enlightenment of Mankind, and waiting for the day when it would be free of the shackles of the organised Church.

Entry into the order was said to be a secret process, and only special, chosen individuals would be admitted. The brotherhood's background and direction were confirmed in 1615 with the publication of the Confessio Fraternitatis, or 'Confession of the Brotherhood,' and the 'Third Chemical Wedding of Christian Rosenkreuz.' These writings created much interest in the movement, and divisions of the order were instigated throughout Europe. It is generally felt that the Rosicrucians may have been one of the precursors to the Freemason fraternity, but how much reality is behind their mythical heritage?

Some sources suggest there may have been some groups similar to the Rosicrucians dating from around the twelfth century AD in Europe and Asia. However, the brotherhood detailed in the texts of the 1610s was purely the fictional work of John Valentin Andrea, a Lutherian philosopher and theologian. Andrea admitted writing the pamphlets as a satire of the prevalent deep interest in mysticism and occultism. By combining contemporary muses of knighthood, far-off lands and romantic notions, it is claimed Andrea was trying to promote anti – Papal Protestant ideas. Certainly, he denounced the whole issue of Rosicrucians as mere folly for the rest of his life; the order's sacred symbol of a rose in the centre of a cross was actually taken from Andrea's own family shield.

But Andrea's work began something he never intended, and the original satirical works ended up being viewed seriously. In the late seventeenth century, new Rosicrucian groups claiming direct descent from those mentioned in Andrea's writings sprang up across Europe. In the mid eighteenth century Rosicrucianism apparently helped to establish the Freemasonry movement. It is said that Saint-Germain the Deathless was instrumental in both organisations and certainly his claimed abilities in alchemy, medicine and transmutation would have been of immense interest to the early followers. The Scottish Masonic movement is believed to have retained many Rosicrucian influences, and in 1866 centres of Masonic Rosicrucianism were created throughout Britain and America.

These Rosicrucian movements have continued to this day largely as a select branch of the Freemason community, and around 1910 Harvey Spencer Lewis founded the 'Ancient Mystical Order Rosae Crucis,' or AMORC, in California. Now generally accepted as being the main world-wide division of the movement, it has followers and lodgers across the world. The AMORC headquarters in San José is believed to be a massive complex that houses a museum, temple, auditorium, planetarium, art gallery and library. Most of their practices are held in the utmost secrecy, and entry into the Order is said to be limited to select, high-achieving freemasons. Many conspiracy theorists claim that other Rosicrucian orders try to entice people into their groups through suggestive advertising and false claims.

The stated aim of AMORC is to encourage the spiritual liberation of people so that individuals can find their own free versions of God. The original idea of reducing the need for organised, church-based religion still persists. Rosicrucian followers are also believed to strive for knowledge in the secrets of nature; in the symbolic properties of art, literature and ancient history and in developing the psychic abilities of Mankind. Critics of the movement claim they promote anti-Christian doctrines. As with many secret organisations, the imaginations of the curious can create theories far more outlandish than the truth. And in this area Rosicrucians are unique, as it seems it was the fiction-driven creative mind of John Andrea that actually instigated the movement in the first place.

Oak Island

IN THE SUMMER of 1795 a young Nova Scotian boy called Daniel McGinnis landed on one of the many small islands in Mahone Bay. He found signs of human inhabitation and an aged ship's tackle block dangling from an old oak tree. Under this tree a slight dip in the ground suggested a hole had been dug and refilled. McGinnis excitedly believed he had stumbled across the site of a buried treasure hoard. He raced home to request the help of his two best friends, John Smith and Anthony Vaughan, and the next day they began digging in the hollow. They discovered a shaft 13 feet wide,

and four feet down they found a platform of foreign flagstones. Ten feet down they found a layer of supporting log beams, and at 20 and 30 feet they found further oaks platforms. The three friends realised they would need more manpower and better equipment, and returned home, eager to raise the funds needed for a more ambitious attempt.

Initially they failed, but in 1803 a local doctor called Simeon Lynds heard of Smith's discoveries on Oak Island and was suitably interested to raise funds from among his friends. The new team dug in earnest and found platforms of logs and clay at ten-foot intervals. By the time they reached the 90-feet mark, the team was removing one bucket of water with every two buckets of mud. Late one evening they found what they thought was the last layer before the treasure. They had the next day off, and spent the time planning how to split their expected wealth. The next Monday morning, however, all but the top thirty feet of the shaft was filled with murky, muddy water. The group tried to bail the water out, but the level remained constant. They tried pumping the water out, but to no avail and abandoned that attempt. In 1805, the group decided to dig another, parallel shaft 110 feet deep, and then tunnel towards the expected treasure chests. But they dug too close to the original shaft, and the wall between the two cracked, filling the new tunnel with hundreds of gallons of water. Out of funds, the work ceased.

No subsequent attempt has been quite so close to rescuing the treasure, but more has become known about the shaft. It was discovered that a carefully constructed underground canal had been built. It ran from the beach, 500 feet away, and entered the shaft's core. This meant that the logs and clay acted as an effective cork, which, once removed, allowed the water to rush into the chamber. Later efforts to drill into the shaft discovered wood from chest casings, loose metal such as coins, decorative metal chains, a layer of concrete, soft metal such as bullion, and even a piece of parchment with writing on it. This real, tangible evidence of treasure, and the obvious efforts of whoever hid it, has helped to promote and encourage continual efforts to raise the bounty.

The question of who owned the treasure has also baffled interested minds. The suggestion that it is Inca gold, hidden as the natives fled from Spanish settlers, has been mooted. There is the idea that it is a cache of British Army war chests, hidden as their forces retreated during the American War of Independence. However, in 1937, a New England businessman, Gilbert D. Heddon, researched the possibility that the wealth belonged to the well-known privateer, Captain William Kidd. Heddon hoped that by reading Kidd's history he would find clues leading to details of a shaft's contents. Like all others, his efforts proved fruitless.

By 1965 Oak Island had turned into a honeycomb of shafts and tunnels, so the American geologist, Bob Dunfield tried a method of brute force to find the treasure. He imported a 70-tonne crane and dug a hole 140 deep and 100 feet wide, but found nothing other than the remnants of earlier searches. In 1970, a new investment group called the Triton Alliance commissioned a complete geological study of the island. The report's findings have never been released to the public, but it enthused the Triton group enough to excavate the site. They began a project called Borehole 10-X, which found pieces of brass, china and wood cribbing 200 feet down, but the project has suffered numerous problems.

Many locals claim that centuries of haphazard searching have left the island in such a mess that the hidden loot will never be found. Others still believe it might be possible to recover the hoard. But, for now at least, it looks as if the secret treasures of Oak Island are safely buried.

THE CURSE OF TUTENKHAMUN

IN THE LATE nineteenth century a young English archaeologist by the name of Howard Carter was convinced that the remains of the 'Boy King,' the pharaoh Tutenkhamun, lay undisturbed somewhere in Egypt. Carter first arrived in Egypt in 1891, and eventually secured funding for his archaeological digs from the wealthy Lord Carnarvon in 1917. After five years of little success, Carnarvon gave Carter one last season of financial support. On 4th November 1922, Carter's team found a step cut into the rock floor of the Valley of the Kings. As they dug and removed the covering material, they discovered a set of steps that ended at a door inscribed with the name 'Tutenkhamun'. Carter ruled that they would do no more digging until Lord Carnarvon reached the site, and immediately sent a telegram back to Britain.

Carnarvon travelled to Egypt and together he and Carter entered the tomb. They discovered a fake room, a storage room and then the burial chamber. Unlike other pharaohs, Tutenkhamun had lain un-disturbed since death, and when Carter had peered in by candlelight he discovered an untold array of treasures. The team cata-logued and recorded all the items they found, the most impressive of which was the king's sarcophagus – three interlocking coffins, the last of which depicted the earthly form of Tutenkhamun in beautiful gold metalwork. Inside this lay the mummified body of the Boy King. Everyone celebrated at

Death mask of Tutenkamun, the 'Boy King' of Egypt.

finding an unplundered tomb, and Carter's team felt vindicated in their search. However, there were rumours that Carter had removed a sign above the tomb door that read 'Death shall come on swift wings to him that toucheth the tomb of the Pharaoh.'

In the spring of 1923, Lord Carnarvon was bitten on the neck by a mosquito. He accidentally cut the bite whilst shaving, and the wound became infected. He started suffering fevers and chills and died shortly

Could the Curse of the Pharoahs have been a virus or poisonous fungus left in the tombs, to infect the unwary?

after in Cairo hospital. It is believed all the lights in the hospital went out when he passed away, and his favourite dog back in England is said to have howled and dropped dead the same instant. The press had a field day, claiming it was the curse of the pharaoh – strangely, when the mummy was unwrapped, it had a bite on the cheek in exactly the same place as Carnarvon's had been. Over the next few years, two of Carnarvon's relatives, Carter's personal secretary and several others connected with the discovery were said to have died in strange circumstances. Each time one died, the British media linked the death to the curse.

Some historians believe that the Ancient Egyptians placed poison inside the tombs to gain vengeance on grave robbers. Scientists have also advanced many theories in recent years that suggest food placed inside the tomb to help the dead body's spiritual journey may actually have helped the breeding of microscopic spores which entered the explorer's lungs when they opened the tomb. This highly volatile fungus, which would have developed uninhibited over 3000 years, then caused terrible fever and fatigue in the bodies it infected. Certainly, Lord Carnarvon, who was not in the best of health, would already have been tired from the long journey out to Egypt and would therefore be more susceptible to infection..

But this theory does not totally explain the supposed curse, because very few of the people who were actually on hand died early. Of the 26 people present at the opening of the burial chamber, only six died in the following ten years. At the sarcophagus opening, 22 were present, of whom six died within a decade, while nobody who helped unwrap the mummified body suffered an early death. Carter himself, at the forefront of all the discoveries, died of natural causes at the age of 66.

However, Carnarvon was the one who funded the search, was and the first on site for the opening so it may be possible that Tutenkhamun focused his ire directly on him. It is certainly true that Cairo's hospital's lights failed at the time of his death, and the story about his dog has never been disproved. One final fascinating rumour was that Carnarvon had given Carter a pet canary as a token of good luck to find the tomb. On the day of its discovery, it is said that a cobra – an animal symbolic of pharaohs – ate the bird. In fact, Carter had it kept alive and well, although it did pass into the possession what could be thought of as another kind of snake – he gave it to a bank manager!

MISCELLANEOUS

Demonic Possession

THEOLOGIANS BELIEVE THE idea of possession began with the Zoroastrian religion in Persia, but the continual references to the phenomenon in the teachings of Christ sealed the concept as a major spiritual occurrence. A survey conducted in 2002 revealed that 54% of Americans believe in the genuine power of unwelcome spiritual forces to control a person. Many people believe the religious aspect of possession refers just to our natural instinct, desires and temptations. Surely other-worldly forces cannot really inhabit the human mind?

Something bizarre does seem happen to people who become fixated with the occult. Possession is believed to happen over a gradual period, and begins with spiritually sensitive people dabbling with strange forces. It can be inflicted by a bad Ouija

Mediaeval engraving of holy men casting out demons.

Belief in possession by demons persists in many parts of the world, even today. These tribesmen are casting out their own particular demons.

board experience, an uncontrolled séance, or by an encounter with a particularly potent ghost or poltergeist. As time passes, so the possessed person gradually loses control over their actions. To begin with, their 'mind-invader' can be pleasant and helpful, but as soon as the host body tells it to leave, it can become hateful and spiteful.

The original partial possession becomes more total. It results in the possessed person being isolated and aggressive. Their behaviour increases in its unpredictability, and they suffer from terrible nightmares, sleeplessness and headaches. Finally, the fear that the spirit's power is uncontrollable can drive the possessed person to attempt suicide, or to be locked in a mental hospital. If caught in time, the possessed person can be exorcised by a priest, but the exertions needed for this have also been known to kill the victim.

In 2002, an American woman called Andrea Yates claimed demonic possession had caused her to kill her five children. Yates drowned the infants aged between six months and seven years in June 2001 and pleaded not guilty by reason of insanity.

Many experts believe possession is nothing more mysterious than being an outlet for severe mental difficulties. Just as Biblical possession may represent impure desires, so real-life possession may represents psychosis. In whichever case, possession is a dangerous state of mind that needs immediate professional help to restore the mental balance of its unfortunate victim.

PERPETUAL MOTION

EVER SINCE THE invention of the wheel, Man has been searching for unlimited energy – the idea of perpetual motion, the notion that once the machine starts turning, it would never stop. The law of physics tell modern scientists that perpetual motion is an impossibility, but engineers from previous times where not governed by such inhibitive rules. Between 1607 and 1903 the British Patent Office received over 600 applications for perpetual motion inventions. However, only one man has dared to suggest he really did conquer the problem.

Johann Ernst Elias Bessler was born in 1680 in Zittau in Saxony. In 1712 he appeared in the town of Gera with a wheel which he claimed was self-moving. With a little push to start, the three-feet-wide, four-inch-thick wheel worked itself up to a regular speed. It could lift a weighted bag and, it was claimed, would continue turning forever. But Bessler seemed to attract many enemies, and very little notice was taken of his invention.

In 1716 Landgrave of Hesse-Cassel became his patron, and it was at his home in 1717

The theory of perpetual motion has engaged the attentions of scientists for centuries.

that Bessler created his greatest wheel. Twelve feet wide and fourteen inches thick, it constantly revolved at 25 or 26 turns a minute. On 12th November 1717 the wheel was locked and sealed in its room. Two weeks later the room was reopened and the wheel was still turning at a constant 25rpm. They sealed it away for a further six weeks, and once more, when viewed, it was revolving at 25 rpm.

Bessler asked for £20,000 to reveal the secrets of his wheel, but nobody seemed ready to provide such a huge amount of money. At the same time, his enemies were casting doubts on his invention, but many learned and official figures who studied the wheels confirmed there was no trickery involved. Bessler grew impatient and vexed and simply disappeared, taking his secret to his grave.

It is said that he left certain clues which, when deciphered, will demonstrate how his amazing machine worked. But until then perpetual motion will have to remain, at least in scientific eyes, a practical impossibility.

Rods

THE RODS PHENOMENON started in March 1994 when Jose Escamilla, a film editor from New Mexico, captured some interesting footage of a UFO sighting. As he studied the tapes in frame-by-frame detail, Escamilla noticed long, thin, bizarre objects darting about the screen. Initially he thought they were birds or insects that were very close to the camera lens, but as he sharpened the clarity of the picture, an elongated cylindrical body could be viewed. Their rod-like shape gave them their name, and in subsequent years, a wealth of similar footage has been recorded from all corners of the globe.

Rods seem to be living organisms, unnoticeable to the human eye because of their rapid movement. They have an extended, ultra-thin frame, and sets of wings or fins protruding from their body. The quick, haphazard motion suggests they are organic life, but detailed analysis is difficult, as they are only discernible in pictures taken with high-shutter-speed cameras. To some extent they look like stick insects with no real limbs, but the possibility that they are known organisms has been proven wrong. Footage of rods moving alongside existing animals highlights the fact that their design and attributes are quite unlike any creature that we recognise.

There has been a huge amount of private footage captured by enthusiasts, but very few examples of truly high-grade, broadcast quality photography. One of the best examples of rods on film came from Mark Lichtle, who was recording parachutists leaping into a cavern in Mexico called the Cave of the Swallows. During the 45 minutes of footage, countless rods can be seen alongside insects, birds and people, and it is now widely accepted that the Cave of the Swallows is one of the best places to capture rods on camera. However, rods are sighted across the world, and even the US Navy is reported to have knowledge and footage of the phenomenon. With an abundance of growing proof, it seems the idea of flying rods has to be taken seriously. But still, nobody has any idea what they truly are.

VOODOO

Notions such as curses, black magic, pin dolls and skeleton-painted priests are inextricably linked with the popular perception of Voodoo. A combination of Hollywood movies, fictional novels and comic book story lines have helped instil the idea that Voodoo is a mysterious, evil religion, stemming from darkest Africa. Many people believe it has been used to bring about the early deaths of unwelcome researchers and to resurrect the zombified bodies of dead believers. However, those who practise Voodoo say these rumours and myths have been borne out of ignorance and misplaced fear. Voodoo, they say, is actually a peaceful religion very similar in emphasis to the Catholic faith. They say it should cause no feeling of trepidation in anybody.

Voodoo, also known as Vodun, Vodoun, Voudou or Sevi Lua, originated in the west African countries of Nigeria, Benin and Togo. 'Voodoo' is an ancient African word for 'Great Spirit,' and the religion itself is believed to stretch back many millennia. The first the developed word knew of it was when slave traders started capturing African workers in the sixteenth century, and deporting them to the West Indies. On arriving in the islands, the slaves were forcibly invested in the Catholic faith, but as there were few facilities for them to actually practise this new religion, many slipped back into their native traditions.

Their religion was founded on the idea of one supreme God – an unknowable but almighty force. Under Him there lies a network of 'Loa' or spirits, which are broadly equivalent to the Christian idea of patron

A spider model commonly used in voodoo ceremonics.

saints. Each Loa represents a different area of life and has certain qualities. For example, if a farmer was worried about his crops he would focus his worship on the Loa known as 'Zaka,' the spirit of agriculture. Despite the similarity between faiths, the French and Spanish masters refused to accept that these enslaved savages could have their own indigenous religion. Fearing that they were actually worshipping the devil, Voodoo was banned, and slave leaders and priests were beaten into confessing that their rituals were evil.

However, the Voodoo faith was continued

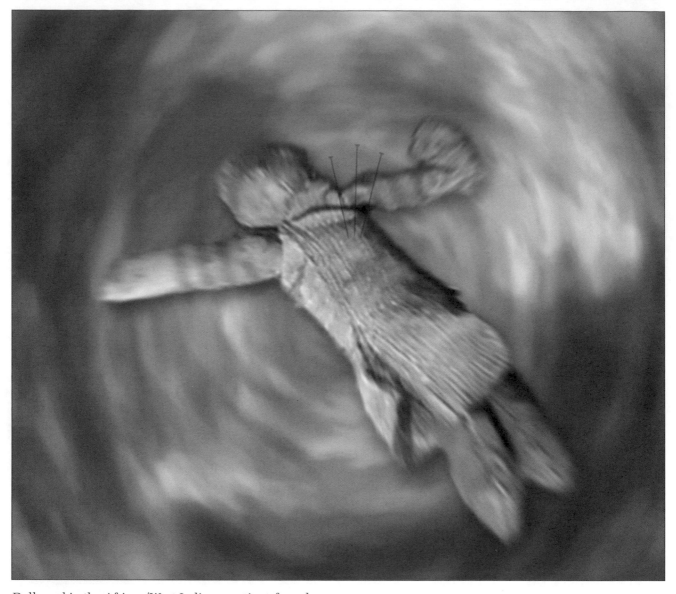

Doll used in the African/West Indian practice of voodoo.

in secret, particularly in Haiti. Over time it even adopted some aspects of the Catholic religion, as descendants of the original slaves spread throughout across the Caribbean. The belief of West Indian workers mixed with Voodoo practices of slaves taken to the American southlands and a centre for the faith was soon created in New Orleans with its fertile blend of French, Spanish and African cultures. Today, 15% of New Orleans citizens, and 60 million people worldwide, practise Voodoo. In 1996 it was also made the official faith of Benin. Despite this, there is still a great deal of mystery and fear attached to Voodoo rituals.

The Voodoo temple is called a 'Hounfour,' and the leader of the ceremony is a male priest called a 'Houngan,' or a female priest called a 'Mambo.' At the centre of the temple there is a post used to contact spirits, and a highly decorated altar. There is a feast before the ceremony, and a particular pattern relating to the Loa being worshipped is outlined on the temple floor. Dancing and chanting accompanied by beats from rattles and religious drums called 'Tamboulas.' Begins. One of the dancers is said to be possessed by the Loa, enters a trance and behaves just as the Loa would. An animal, normally a chicken, goat, sheep or dog, is sacrificed and their blood is collected. This is used to sate the hunger of the Loa.

Although these rites and rituals are used for good purposes – asking for guidance and help – there are some less wholesome practices. Voodoo black magic is performed by 'Caplatas' or 'Bokors' who place curses, and stick pins in Voodoo dolls to cause people pain and suffering. However, this use of Voodoo is very rare, and the faith is promoted by its followers as being a wonderful way to understand the human condition and the world around us. Even though some of the practices seem a little strange, are they really much different from evangelist rituals or even archaic Catholic rites? As with many of Humanity's mysteries, a little tolerance and understanding goes a long way to revealing the truth.

ZOMBIES

THE CENTRE OF THE zombie world is the island of Hispaniola, in the West Indies. Many peasant workers there believe that evil sorcerers called 'bokors' have the power to bring their dead loved-ones back to life as unthinking puppets. The bokors are then said to use these unfortunates as their slaves. It is true that this Caribbean idea of zombies does exist, and that 'zombies' can be found regularly walking the streets of the islands. Some people know members of their family or friends who have been turned into zombies, and as a precaution many poor peasant workers place heavy stone tablets on top of their loved-ones' coffins to stop bokors snatching the bodies.

The reality is truly frightening, although it does not involve otherworldly powers. Psychiatric experts agree that the people identified as zombies by Haitian folk do have problems and suffer from a variety of serious mental health disorders. Some commentators have suggested that the idea of zombies was the way in which Haitian culture could explain these naturally unwell people. Others think it is something much more sinister. It is believed that by using natural, native resources, Haitian bokors can actually induce these mental illnesses.

Using a chemical called tetrodotoxin, a nerve agent found in puffer fish, the bokor's victim can be afflicted with a deep paralysis. The victim's family thinks he or she is dead, and so they are buried. The lack of oxygen in the coffin contributes to brain damage, and when the bokor comes to steal the body, the victim is revived using a substance called datura stramonium, or 'zombie cucumber,' which is also a mind-control drug. Other poisons, like that found in a local cane toad, can be extracted and will act as hallucinogens and anaesthetics on the unfortunate victims. It keeps them in a permanent state of trance, appearing impervious to physical pain, and acts as a warning to other islanders to be wary of the power of bokors.